The Road to Power

Fast Food for
the Soul

The Road to Power

Fast Food for the Soul

Barbara Berger

NEW AMERICAN LIBRARY

New American Library
Published by New American Library, a division of
Penguin Putnam Inc., 375 Hudson Street,
New York, New York 10014, U.S.A.
Penguin Books Ltd, 80 Strand,
London WC2R 0RL, England
Penguin Books Australia Ltd, Ringwood,
Victoria, Australia
Penguin Books Canada Ltd, 10 Alcorn Avenue,
Toronto, Ontario, Canada M4V 3B2
Penguin Books (N.Z.) Ltd, 182–190 Wairau Road,
Auckland 10, New Zealand

Penguin Books Ltd, Registered Offices:
Harmondsworth, Middlesex, England

Published by New American Library, a division of Penguin Putnam Inc.
First published in Denmark in 1995 by BeamTeam Books.

First Printing, March 2002
10 9 8 7 6 5 4 3 2 1

 REGISTERED TRADEMARK—MARCA REGISTRADA

LIBRARY OF CONGRESS CATALOGING-IN-PUBLICATION DATA:

Berger, Barbara (Barbara W.)
    Fast food for the soul : the road to power / Barbara Berger
    p. cm.
    "First published in Denmark in 1995 by Beam Team Books"—T.p. verso
    ISBN 0-451-50554-5 (alk. paper)
    1. Success. I. Title.
  BJ1611.2B46 2002
  158—dc21

        00-009544

Set in Hiroshige Book

Printed in the United States of America

BOOKS ARE AVAILABLE AT QUANTITY DISCOUNTS WHEN USED TO PROMOTE PRODUCTS
OR SERVICES. FOR INFORMATION PLEASE WRITE TO PREMIUM MARKETING DIVISION,
PENGUIN PUTNAM INC., 375 HUDSON STREET, NEW YORK, NEW YORK 10014.

To Tim, Mark, and Robin

Contents

1	The Road to Power	1
2	The Power of the Force	7
3	The Power of Affirmation	13
4	The Power of Release	21
5	The Power of NO	31
6	The Power of Visualization	39
7	The Power of Alpha	51
8	The Power of Focus	61
9	The Power of Secrecy	77
10	The Power of Money	79
11	The Power of Giving	89
12	The Power of Love	95
13	The Power of Silence	101
14	The Power of Nature	107
15	The Power of Eating Less	113
16	The Power of Exercise	119
17	The Power of Praise and Blessing	127
18	The Power of Friends	137
19	The Power of Fast Food for the Soul	143

Chapter 1

The Road to Power

We are what we think.
We become what we believe.
Our life is what we visualize.
Our life is what we say it is.

We can change our lives
by changing our thoughts.

This is a book about power.
  This is a book about the ways in which you can control your life and create the life you've always wanted to live.

Our thoughts and words are all-powerful.
Through our thoughts and words,
we create our lives.
We are the only ones who have complete control
over our thoughts and words
because we are the only thinkers in our minds.
This is why we are so powerful.

The Revolution in Consciousness

This is the great revolution in consciousness that is taking place right now. More and more people are claiming their own power. More and more people are awakening to the simple fact that what they think, declare, and focus on is what they attract into their lives.

We are only victims of our own thinking.

If your life is not working, it's time to look at your attitudes and thoughts because only here will you find the key to taking control of your life and changing your destiny.

Decide on the life you want, visualize it, affirm it, decree it, focus on it, believe it, have faith in it, and you will find yourself living this life much sooner and much faster than you ever dreamed possible.

The Way the Mind Works

When you realize what it's all about, it's almost too simple to be true. It's almost a joke.

When the realization dawns on you, and you stop laughing, you'll probably ask yourself why you spent so much of your life working so hard, struggling like mad against outside circumstances, when all you had to do was change your own thinking.

The outside world is just a manifestation of

what we choose to think about. Focus on sickness, poverty, and misery, and you will experience these things instantly. Change your focus and concentrate on the feast of life, on your blessings, on all the Good in life, on vibrant health and the abundance of the universe—and instantly they will appear for you.

What changed? The universe surely didn't. All that changed was your thinking.

The Power of Inner Work

Look around you. Most people are struggling desperately every day to survive or to perform, achieve, and succeed.

So many of us also find ourselves rushing around madly, because we believe that the harder we try, the more worthy we will become as human beings.

I know, I've been there myself. I was brought up that way, just like you were. I had the same education and heard all the same arguments we created to justify struggle. For example: That's the way the world is. You have to work hard to make it. Money doesn't grow on trees. Life is a struggle. If I work hard enough, maybe they'll love me. Old age means sickness and misery, etc.

Believing this, we desperately try to force our Good on the outer plane. Until sooner or later, we realize that it just doesn't work like that. We cannot force our Good on the outer plane.

The real point of power is inside.

So do the inner work. Examine your thoughts and attitudes, dump the ones that don't work, and adopt the focus that will create the life you want to live.

And leave the outer plane alone.

The outer plane will take care of itself. It's like a magical computer printout of your life: anytime you press the print command, it will give you an exact reading of what you are thinking on the inner plane.

So forget struggle. Forget hardship. Forget poverty, sickness, and unhappiness. Do the inner work and start enjoying your life right now.

Practical Techniques

Since this is a book about power, each chapter contains practical techniques you can use in your daily life to gain control of your life and create the life you want to live. All the techniques described in this book have helped me improve the quality of my life at one time or another. I felt moved to write this book because these techniques helped me so much, I want to share them with you.

I tried to design this book so it's easy to use. I wrote this for busy people and for people who have little patience with long-winded intellectual discussions and/or long, boring explanations. If you want fast results, if you want techniques that are easy to understand, easy to learn, and work quickly, this book should be fun for you.

For several reasons:

First of all, this is a short book.

And second, you don't have to read the book from start to finish to make it work for you. You can just dive in to any chapter that attracts you and start there. Just follow your intuition . . . then this book will be happy with you too!

I've also found that different techniques have worked for me at different times of my life and that the methods I use also keep changing according to the situation, the problem, or the needs of the moment. Again, I try to follow my intuition and use whatever technique feels right.

We are all constantly evolving, growing, and changing, so we outgrow techniques or we get tired of them and release them for a while so we can move on to new methods. Likewise, a technique that worked well for us in the past can suddenly start to appeal to us again, even though we haven't used it for months or years. Then we go back and reconsider it and find new meaning, new depth, and new power. Our understanding of different techniques and ideas will constantly evolve for us, like peeling off the layers of an onion, as we continue to grow and gain power over our lives.

And finally, everything in this book is meant to give you great pleasure and a deep sense of joy. I believe that when we connect to our Higher Selves and understand that we are responsible for our lives and destinies, we see life as the great adventure it truly is and can consciously claim our own power to become the true creators we in fact already are.

Chapter 2

The Power of the Force

Whatever we human beings choose to call it, our universe, our existence, our actions, our evolution are guided by a higher principle, intelligence, or power.

This power or force has a lot of different names, such as:

God
Life
The Force
The Life Force
The God Force
The Creator
Brahman
Allah
Tao
Jehovah
Our Heavenly Father
The First Cause
The Life Principle

I AM That I AM
The Presence
The Supreme Being
The Divine Presence
The Animating Principle
The Cosmic Mind
The Living Spirit
The Higher Self
    . . . just to name a few.

Recognize the Force and Stop Resisting

When you recognize the Force and stop resisting the nature of human evolution, you will find that your entire life changes. When you realize that you are 100 percent responsible for everything that happens in your life, that your Higher Self in fact designed your life for your own soul growth, and that every difficulty you meet on your pathway through life is part of your learning process, you will experience a feeling of relief, elation, and true liberation.

You will understand that all struggle on the outer plane solves nothing. You will see that we are not victims of anything. There are no accidents in life and no victims.

Life is a game we cannot lose because we are all here to evolve, no matter what happens.

In fact, life on Planet Earth is like going to

school. This is our classroom, which we designed ourselves for our own benefit. And struggle is only a sign that we are resisting, that we are not yet doing the inner work we must do sooner or later to move on to the next stage of our evolution.

But, of course, there is no rush. You can resist as long as you want to . . . because there is an infinity of time . . . and sooner or later, you will get it.

The Universe Is Your Source

Everything in your life, my life, and everyone else's life comes from the infinite universe. The infinite universe or the God Force is the source and provides us with everything. And since there is an infinite, endless supply of matter and energy, how can we lack?

Poverty is really the failure to recognize the infinite universe as the source of everything. Other people are not your source, nor is your job, the welfare society, the government, your family, or outside circumstances. None of these things are the source of your life, wealth, or prosperity. Other people and situations are the channels through which the abundance of the universe manifests in your life . . . but they are not the source.

Open Your Heart and Mind to the True Source

So recognize the true source of all life and abundance and open your heart and mind to greater Good, greater prosperity, increased health, abundance, peace, and joy in your life. It is always available. It is always there, just waiting for your recognition. So stop limiting your Good, your health, or your wealth by limiting your ideas or stating that you can only receive from fixed channels. For example, don't say that you live on a fixed income (in other words, on your salary) because by doing so, you are closing the doors to the source of infinite supply. Realize, affirm, and visualize your Good coming to you through an unlimited number of channels from the infinite universe.

Affirm daily: I am now open and receptive to my Highest Good. The unlimited supply of the universe now pours forth to me from an unlimited number of channels. I give thanks for the infinite blessings and outpouring of abundance that are now manifesting in my life.

What is true abundance?

True abundance is all the Good
the universe holds for us:

Love
Peace
Radiant Health
Financial Prosperity
Time
Beauty
Spiritual Growth
Friends
Family
Music and Art
Joy
Nature
Wisdom and Understanding
and an infinity of more . . .

Why settle for less?

Chapter 3

The Power of Affirmation

Do you know your word is law?

That what you say, even casually, becomes your reality?

I am quite sure people would be much more careful of what they say if they were aware of the power of the spoken word.

You see, every word you speak or write is an affirmation.

To affirm is literally *to make firm*.

To affirm is to manifest your thoughts into material form.

Unfortunately, far too many people, not realizing the power of their words, are affirming lack, poverty, illness, and unhappiness for themselves. By complaining and proclaiming misery, they are decreeing and creating the very misery, lack, pain, and sorrow they so dislike.

Take Control of Your Words

You are the only person in your mind. You can decide, right now, to take control of your words, both written and spoken, and thereby take control of your destiny. After all, you and no one else is responsible for what comes out of your mouth. No one else can force you to speak words of negativity. It's your decision. So if you want to change your life, take responsibility for your own words right now.

Once you become aware of the power of words, you can quickly see why other people's lives are as they are. Just listen to what they are saying, to their conversations. It's very revealing. People who complain all the time, who focus on misery, who are always moaning and groaning about how difficult their lives are, really do have difficult lives. *Their lives are as they decree them to be.*

Those who proclaim joy, success, and love, those who speak positive words, who decree that good things are happening, live joyful, successful, interesting, loving lives.

"In the Beginning Was the Word. . . ."[1]

The Bible and other ancient scriptures all speak of the power of the word. They teach that our words are the creative force of the universe, alive with power for good or for evil.

Many modern psychological techr
recognize the power of our words. For example,
neuro-linguistic programming, an effective technique for reprogramming our mental states, helps
people change their behavioral patterns. An important tool in NLP for understanding behavioral
programs is listening to what people say.

Mantras, or the use of sacred words, also aim
to reprogram our minds and bodies to increased
health and happiness through repeating words of
power.

The world-famous mantra below was created
by the French physician Emile Coué (1857–1926)
to help people heal themselves of all kinds of illnesses and psychological problems. Coué, who
was a medical doctor in Nancy, France, successfully treated thousands of patients with this
mantra. All one has to do is repeat it aloud, fifteen
times in a row, three times a day, each and every
day. Repetition helps the mantra work on our subconscious mind, which then acts accordingly,
without interference from our logical intellect.

Every day in every way
I am getting better and better.[2]
EMILE COUÉ

Proclaim Your Affirmations Aloud Every Day

You can develop positive affirmations for every area of your life. You can also use affirmations created by other people, like the Coué affirmation. Or you can use passages from sacred texts, the Bible, or, better yet, you can create your own affirmations.

Start with those areas in your life that are most pressing and begin affirming the positive outcome you want to experience. Decree life as you want it to be and believe it should be. Always affirm in the present tense. It doesn't matter if your affirmations are not yet true (have not yet manifested in the outer world). By affirming positive outcomes, you create them, first in your subconscious mind and in the universal mind, then in the outer world. Your words and your belief in your decrees make them manifest on the physical plane.

Repeat Your Affirmations 15 Times in a Row

I suggest saying your affirmations every morning and evening aloud for about five minutes at a time. If you have time during the middle of the day, say your affirmations again.

Many teachers and healers also suggest repeating each of your important affirmations fifteen times in a row, to energize yourself and give your affirmation the necessary power.

Repeating the Lord's Prayer out loud fifteen times in a row is a very powerful general affirmation.

Writing Affirmations

When you find yourself in situations where you can't say your affirmations aloud (for example, at your office, on the train), write them down in your notebook. Writing affirmations fifteen times in a row is also a powerful way to manifest Good in your life.

Be Specific

Not only should you change your affirmations to meet your evolving needs, you should not hesitate to be specific in your affirmations. It's fine to use general affirmations on a daily basis, but for specific needs and situations, be bold and affirm the results you want.

For example, to increase your income and meet your financial obligations, be definite about prosperity. (See Chapter 10 on The Power of Money.) Affirm:

I am a rich child of the infinite universe. Abundant supply now manifests in my life and I now meet my financial obligations easily and effortlessly. _____ (state amount) now comes quickly to me.

For health problems, you can create your own specific affirmations to meet specific needs or use general affirmations such as the examples below for health and healing:

My body is strong and healthy. Every day, new life, strength, and vitality are flowing to every atom, cell, and organ of my body. Every day in every way I am getting better and better and better.

I love my body and give thanks for its perfect functioning. Every cell and atom of my body now radiate vibrant health and vitality.

I give thanks for ever-increasing health, strength, and vitality. I am enjoying radiant good health now.

Affirm and Demonstrate!

As you continue to affirm, you will see the results of your inner work begin to manifest in the world around you. You will experience surprising demonstrations, unexpected changes, new Good, and an increased sense of control over your destiny.

As you begin to experience the power of your words, you can expand this power for Good by affirming Good for other people too. Often your affirmations of Good for another person can turn the tide in their life. Especially when their need seems great, do not be afraid to speak bold words of affirmation to them directly. Say things like:

You will be fine.
Everything is okay.
You are just fine the way you are.
Of course you can do it.
I know you can do it.
I have complete faith in you.
I predict complete success for you in this venture.
I admire your talents and ability.
You are strong and healthy.
You look so much better today.
Thank you for the inspiration you've given me.
I really appreciate your help.

Such words can make all the difference to the people around you, whether they be troublesome acquaintances, good friends, co-workers, family members, children, or lovers. (See Chapter 17 on The Power of Praise and Blessing.)

Affirm and Enjoy!

Continue to play with your affirmations!

Sing them, chant them, dance to them, write them down, hang them on your walls, paste them on your refrigerator and telephones, hang them in your bathroom, repeat them silently to yourself throughout the day. I promise you that soon you will realize the full power of your words to create the Good that you so rightfully desire and deserve!

Chapter 4

The Power of Release

One of the best ways to feel better is to release.

We're all carrying around such incredibly heavy loads of excess baggage, stuff we don't need, stuff that's weighing us down and preventing our Good from manifesting.

When you release, you become lighter. Releasing is a good way to raise your energy.

There are different ways of releasing:

Mental/emotional release
Physical release

Mental/Emotional Releasing

When we harbor negative emotions toward people, places, things, situations, or events, we are actually linking ourselves to them with an almost unbreakable bond. You can be on the other side of the world, but if you hate someone, you are linked to that person as if you were sitting in the same room, battling each other.

Who do such negative emotions hurt?

You!

You are the person who suffers because you're the one who's carrying around the negative emotions. You're the one who's being eaten up inside. Not only do negative emotions make you feel bad, they can actually make you physically ill and manifest in the end as ulcers, heart disease, high blood pressure, and cancer, just to name a few of the more obvious ones.

So not only is releasing a great way to make yourself feel better, you can even heal yourself of serious illness by releasing the negative emotions you have toward people, places, things, situations, events, and so on.

What Is Releasing?

Releasing is not a question of forgiving, although truly forgiving is probably even better than releasing, though harder to do. By releasing I mean just that: *You let go.* Releasing is not an intellectual exercise. You don't have to forgive the person or event, nor do you have to explain to yourself why or how or if the act of release is justified. You just do it.

By releasing or letting go, you avoid arguing with yourself, so it's an especially good way to free yourself from those people you are having a hard time forgiving.

In other words, releasing is something you are doing for your own Good, for your own health and well-being, not for anyone else. You don't practice release because you are trying to be noble. When you release, you do it simply because you know that if you can let things go, if you can release negative emotions, you are going to feel a whole lot better. So all you have to do is make the decision to release and do it on a regular basis.

Remember to Release First

It's interesting to note that often people who are working with positive affirmations (see Chapter 3 on The Power of Affirmation) don't get the results they're seeking until they start releasing. This is because when we hold on to negative emotions, they do more than just bring us down, make us sick, and clutter up our minds; negative emotions fill up so much space in our lives that they can block our Good from coming to us. And when we work with positive affirmations, we are striving to manifest new Good in our lives.

You can practice releasing by proclaiming aloud or by writing any of the affirmations of release listed below.

Good Statements of Release

Some of my favorite statements for releasing troublesome people from your life:

I completely release you, ____.
I release you and let you go to your Highest Good.

I completely and absolutely release you, ____.
I bless you with love and release you.

I completely and wholeheartedly release you, ____, to your Highest Good.

Sometimes we feel intuitively that troublesome people are also holding on to us, so we can also affirm for them:

____, you completely and absolutely release me. You relax and let me go.

____, you completely and wholeheartedly let me go. All things are in harmony between us, now and forever.

If a situation or event is bothering you, you can say:

I completely and wholeheartedly release ____ (situation, condition, relationship, experience, or event). I relax and release it.

I now let go of any conditions or relationships in my life which are no longer for my Highest Good. I now completely let them go and they now completely let me go—for the Highest Good of all.

Releasing People You Love

Releasing the people we love is often the most important type of releasing we can do. Love of children or love of a partner that becomes possessive or that makes us try to dominate and control the other person in the name of love is always damaging. True love means liberation and frees the people we love to grow and evolve in whatever way is best for them.

For example, we might need to release a beloved son or daughter to his or her Highest Good in whatever way is best for the child, and not for us. This type of release not only brings peace and harmony in every case, it will strengthen our relationship with anyone who is near and dear to us.

In cases where you need to release someone dear to you, you might want to say:

_____, I completely and wholeheartedly let
you go to your Highest Good. I love you but
I let you go. You are completely free and I
am completely free. Perfect harmony is the
one and only reality between us.

Releasing Problems or Situations

Sometimes we need to release a problem or situation that has been bothering us for a long time.
We might be spending a great deal of emotional
and mental energy thinking and worrying about
something, when what we really need to do is release it. By letting go of the problem or situation,
we free it to work itself out in whatever way is
best. All our thinking and worrying actually pre-
vent the situation from resolving itself.

In cases like this you can say:

I now completely and wholeheartedly re-
lease _____ (name the problem or situation).
I allow it to work itself out for the Highest
Good of all concerned.

Physical Releasing

To make space for new Good in your life, it's
also important to release things on the physical
plane. We all have a tendency to collect things
even if we no longer need them or use them.

If you have a physical, mental, or emotional

problem, I highly recommend releasing as much as you possibly can, also on the material plane. Let go of clothes, papers, books, furniture, and other items that you no longer use or that no longer please you. You can release them either by giving them to other people who can use them or by just throwing them away. Do whatever seems right, but let as much go as possible.

As you release old possessions, you will find yourself stirring up old energy and old emotions. It can be quite a dramatic and interesting experience. For many people, releasing possessions can be a real eye-opener. As you release, you can thank these items for serving you so well and then send them on to serve someone else. After all, everything in the universe is energy and energy doesn't like to be trapped or to stagnate. Energy likes to circulate. And you will feel better when you help it circulate.

All sickness is
basically congestion.

All healing is
basically circulation.

Releasing Attracts New Good
Not only will cleaning up your clutter make you feel better, creating new space or emptiness in

your life is a good way of attracting new Good, new things, new energy, and new people into your life. It makes sense, doesn't it? Because if your life is too filled up, how will there be room enough for new Good?

Releasing, both mentally and physically, also stimulates creativity. When you let go of old stuff, old ideas and things, new ideas come pouring in. Somehow just creating the mental space for new ideas attracts them. So don't worry if after releasing people, thoughts, and things from your life, you feel completely blank or empty for a while. It's this very emptiness that is a sure sign that new Good is on its way to you. Emptiness always comes right before you get your best new ideas. Emptiness is the vacuum that attracts new Good.

Releasing Relationships

It can be the same with relationships. We can love and respect people and still outgrow them. This is not the same as rejection—we are just evolving, and people don't always evolve in the same way or in the same direction at the same time. In fact, we should thank and bless the people who have shared time, energy, experiences, and space with us on the planet, but this doesn't mean that we cannot and should not move on. When we release people with love so that everyone involved can continue to evolve in whatever way is best for them, we also make space for new relationships and new people in our lives.

When in Doubt, Release

So when you are in doubt about something, when you feel troubled, when you face problems you cannot seem to solve or resolve, or when you have an illness which lingers on, practice releasing each and every day. The results are sure to amaze you.

General Statements of Release

I let go of all fear.
I let go of all anxiety.
I let go of all pain.
I let go of all doubt.
I let go of all sorrow.
I let go of all tension.
I let go of all sadness.
I let go of my resistance to change.
I let go of all anger.
I let go of all guilt.
I let go of all criticism.
I let go of all unforgiveness.
I let go of all hurt.
I let go of all blame.
I let go of all resentment.

I let go of my negative patterns.
I let go of my negative thoughts.
I let go of all struggle.
I let go of old patterns.
I let go of all limitations.
I let go of my negative beliefs.
I let go of the pattern in my consciousness that created this negative condition.
I let go of ____ (name the thing, for example, this apartment, this job, this relationship, etc.).
I bless ____ (name the thing or situation) with love and let it go.
I let go of the past.
I let go of the future.
I let go of my fears about ____.

Choose those statements that suit your needs best and say them aloud fifteen times in a row many times a day. Or repeat them to yourself silently fifteen times or write them down in your notebook fifteen times in a row. Speaking words of release aloud is the most powerful, but silent or written affirmations are also effective, especially when you're at work or in a situation (for example, right before your next meeting) where it's difficult to walk around saying aloud, "I release all fear and doubt. I release all tension," fifteen times in a row!

Chapter 5

The Power of NO

Since what we focus on increases, when we focus on the negative, we give it our power. And thus it grows.

By denying the negative, by refusing to give it our attention, we remove our power from it—and it will wither for lack of attention.

If you affirm, as Catherine Ponder suggests,

Only the Good is real
All else fades away.[1]

you will soon realize that you do not want to give your power or attention to any type of negative input.

Say No to Complaining

When you listen to people's conversations, you find that most people are complaining about something most of the time. If it's not money problems or the weather, it's their health, their children, or their relationships. And by speaking constantly of lack and difficulties, they create more lack and difficulty for themselves.

Refuse to speak of lack or difficulties. Refuse to support negative emotions and fears in yourself or others. Pull back. Don't participate. If you can't express your feelings out loud, at least say silently to yourself: *No. No. No. I do not accept this as true.*

People will get tired of complaining—at least to you—if you don't support their complaints or participate in the conversation.

If you're brave, you can say you don't believe it's true. You might gently point out something that is good and try to shift the focus of the conversation to something positive. Why not ask instead:

Tell me every good thing that happened
to you today!

Even more important:

Don't complain yourself. Don't give your power
to negative emotions and negative words.

Every word you speak is an affirmation. Your word is law. Your words are your affirmations for your life. So what you decree and proclaim (say aloud) for yourself quite literally becomes your reality. So beware!

Don't dwell on your difficulties, problems, or aches and pains. Refuse to speak about them. Refuse to give them any notice. Refuse to give them your power. Instead, when people ask you how you're doing, tell them something good. You can always find something good to focus on and report. And when you do, this Good will grow, especially if you speak of it, proclaim it, and praise it.

If you can't find something good to say, then at least you can keep quiet. Silence is another way of saying no to the negative. By not speaking of problems and difficulties, you give them no power.

Say No to Gossip

Refuse to gossip, criticize, or speak negatively about other people.

If you praise people, even difficult or irritating people, amazing things often happen. This is especially true when you praise people who really bother you. It is as if your positive words reach them on the subconscious level, giving power to the Good in them. Again, what we focus on grows.

It works like this: When we expect people to be

troublesome, they usually are. If we instead focus on their good sides, our encounters with them usually turn out to be surprisingly pleasant.

Say No to Violent, Negative Input from the Media

If we allow ourselves to be bombarded with negative input from the media—violent movies, depressing television programs, neurotic stories and articles, sad tales of woe and horror—how can we expect the Good to grow? Your time is precious and what you focus your attention on is also precious, because whatever you focus on grows. So don't give your power to violence and/or negative thought forms.

Say No to Talk of Lack

As mentioned in Chapter 10 on The Power of Money, people attract lack into their lives by complaining and focusing on their lack of money, their debts, their insufficient salaries, the high level of taxes, the high cost of living, etc. Say no to such talk of lack. Refuse to give your power to such thoughts. Instead, when people talk of lack, say (at least silently to yourself if you can't say it aloud) that you don't believe them.

Say either aloud or to yourself: "We live in an abundant, infinite universe. There is an infinite, unlimited supply of everything in this universe, including money. There is an everlasting abundance of resources in this world and money enough for everyone."

Say No to Illness

The same goes for illness. Refuse to give it any power. If you focus on every little ache and pain, every little ache and pain will grow. It's like the story Deepak Chopra tells in his book *Creating Health*.

A woman goes to the hospital with pains in her side, thinking it's a gallbladder attack. The doctors, including Chopra, open her up and discover cancer, which has spread everywhere. They close her up because they can do nothing for her. When Chopra tells her daughter after the operation, the daughter says, "Doctor, promise me you won't tell my mother. She'll die right away if she knows she has cancer." He agrees not to tell her.

The woman is discharged from the hospital and Chopra never expects to see her again. To Chopra's great surprise, she returns thirteen months later for a checkup. A thorough examination reveals no trace of cancer. When he tells her she's in perfect health, she says, "Doctor, after you removed my gallbladder, I decided I'd never be sick again."[2]

So what is sickness anyway?

And why do some people get sick and die, while others recover and prosper?

Belief creates biology.[3]
NORMAN COUSINS

Our Mental States Control Our Bodies

Our bodies and our immune systems are strongly influenced by our mental states. Scientists have proven that depressed thoughts weaken our immune system. Happy thoughts strengthen us.

Norman Cousins describes in his famous book, *Anatomy of an Illness As Perceived by the Patient*, what happened to him. He had an incurable disease. The doctors told him he was going to die very soon. He was so depressed that he checked into a hotel in Chicago and rented all the funny videos he could think of—all his favorites, like Groucho Marx films. Then he lay in bed and watched the movies and laughed his head off for three weeks. Without his noticing it, his incurable disease disappeared, to the great surprise of his doctors, himself, and everyone else.[4]

The revolution we call
mind-body medicine was

> *based on this simple*
> *discovery: Wherever thought*
> *goes, a chemical goes with it.*[5]
> DEEPAK CHOPRA

In *Ageless Body, Timeless Mind,* Chopra continues: "We must conclude that the body is capable of producing *any* biochemical response once the mind has been given the appropriate suggestions. . . . if we could effectively trigger the intention . . . the body would carry it out automatically."[6]

Say No to Negative Thinking

Most people find it even more difficult to refuse to think negatively. But this too is extremely important, especially in the face of difficulties. Saying no to negative thinking is imperative.

The Ten-Day Mental Diet

Here's one good technique I found in Anthony Robbins' book *Awaken the Giant Within.* For ten days, it is forbidden to dwell upon any negative, unresourceful, or fearful thought for more than one minute. When you catch yourself thinking about something negative or fearful, you must force yourself to focus on something that is positive or happy.[7]

If you dwell on the negative for more than one minute, you have to start the Ten-Day Mental Diet over again.

This Mental Diet is great fun. I suggest you try it right away. It's a real eye-opener.

Chapter **6**

The Power of Visualization

Our power to think, conceive, imagine, and create mental images is working all the time. Whether we are aware of it or not, we are constantly picturing or seeing things in our mind's eye. We are "visualizing."

The implications of this phenomenon are enormous.

Have you noticed that people who are depressed, who think negatively, who see (imagine or visualize) gloom, doom, despair, and failure everywhere they look, usually lead gloomy, desperate lives? And that bright, cheerful people who think positively and picture (imagine) positive outcomes to events are usually successful and happy?

> *Whatever the mind of man*
> *can conceive and believe*
> *it can achieve.*[1]
> NAPOLEON HILL

The Good News

The good news is this: We can learn to harness our power to see, picture, and imagine to create the lives we want to live.

We are all using this picturing power all the time, but most people are picturing or imagining quite unconsciously. In other words, they are not aware of what they are doing. They are not aware that they are continually imagining and picturing for themselves, for other people, and for the world in general. And if they are aware, chances are they are not aware of how powerful an effect this process of "mental picturing" has on their lives. This is very unfortunate because so many people use this power to imagine or visualize to see pain, suffering, and failure for themselves when, with a little training, they could unleash the power of their imaginations to create greater Good.

Picturing Affects Your Health

Not only that, our power to picture or imagine also affects our health. This is because, as scientists have now proved, every thought we think creates or triggers a biochemical reaction in our bodies. This is why so many teachers in the human potential movement, such as José Silva, O. Carl Simonton, Louise L. Hay, Bernie Siegel, Wayne W. Dyer, Stuart Wilde, Deepak Chopra, and others, teach that if we can learn to trigger or program ourselves and our subconscious minds with positive intentions, our bodies will automatically carry out these intentions. Unfortunately, most people do the opposite. But it is important to remember: "Intention is the active partner of attention. Our past intentions create obsolete programming that seems to have control over us. In truth, the power of intention can be reawakened at any time . . . and you can consciously program your mind . . . using the power of your intention."[2] (Deepak Chopra from his book *Ageless Body, Timeless Mind.*)

Blueprints for Life

Our thoughts and pictures are the blueprints we place in our subconscious minds, and our lives are a fulfillment of these thoughts, concepts, and pictures, whether they are positive or negative. Our lives on the outer plane are, in fact, nothing more than the physical manifestation of what is going on in our minds.

Persistent thoughts about sickness
create sickness.

Persistent thoughts about health
create health.

It's Just Your Imagination

Haven't you heard people say, "It's all in your mind," or "It's just your imagination"? Well, there's more truth to this than most people realize. And if it *is* just our imaginations, if our imaginations are such a powerful force that we can create health and happiness for ourselves by training our imagination to picture our Good, then surely we've discovered one of the most powerful tools ever for improving life on Planet Earth!

So why not decide, right now, that whenever you catch yourself "picturing" a negative outcome for yourself or others, you consciously change your mental image and picture something good happening. Once you start watching your thoughts—your inner mental chatter—you might be surprised by what you discover.

Someone once said that 99 percent of what we think today is a repetition of what we thought yesterday. And if you are picturing negative outcomes . . . that sounds pretty serious, doesn't it?

Besides beginning to become aware of your inner dialogue and consciously trying to change it to the positive, you can do specific exercises to train and develop your ability to picture successful outcomes and to reprogram yourself, your body, and your behavior.

Visualization Exercise

Here is an example of a simple, basic visualization exercise that you can practice on a daily basis. There are many such exercises; this one just outlines the general procedure. The most important thing is to find a method you feel comfortable with and to start doing it on a regular basis.

Remember: Practice makes perfect. Your thoughts are a pool of water that has turned muddy because of all your negative thoughts and pictures. By adding clear, fresh water (new, positive thoughts and pictures), your pool will slowly get clearer and clearer. It takes a while, but sooner or later you will start to notice changes in your thinking, in your behavior, and then finally in your life.

For best results, especially if you're just starting, do the same visualization exercise every day for thirty days in a row. This is about the amount of time it takes for the subconscious mind to accept new pictures. After thirty days, you can change your focus to another subject or area of your life.

Step One: Relax

There are many ways to relax. (See Chapter 7 on The Power of Alpha.) Whatever method you prefer, the goal is to release mental and muscular tension, relax in mind and body, let go and slow down your brain waves so you enter the alpha state and open your subconscious mind to new, positive pictures and ideas. When you are relaxed, go to step two.

Step Two: Visualize

What do you want to work on? What area of your life is most pressing right now? Is it better health, success at work, a better relationship? Whatever it is, once you feel relaxed, you should create a mental picture of the positive outcome you desire.

Picture, for example, the situation or state of health you desire, in as many details as possible. *Very important: Always do your picturing in the present tense because the subconscious mind knows no past or future.* So your positive outcome should always be happening *right now*! If you visualize the outcome in the future, your outcome will always remain in the future! So see, visualize, imagine the situation you desire now, in as many details as possible. Feel the pleasure, feel the emotions your new Good will produce within you. Good health makes you feel good, doesn't it? A better relationship with your boss makes you feel relaxed and satisfied, doesn't it? Let yourself *feel* the emotions. Allow yourself to enjoy yourself and your new Good!

When you have pictured your new Good for a few minutes, let the muscles in your eyelids lighten up. Then open your eyes slowly and become aware of the room around you. You can reinforce the exercise by affirming aloud: "I am now fully awake and happier and healthier than ever before." Then resume your regular activities.

For best results, try to do the exercise every day.

The Wheel of Fortune Technique

Catherine Ponder introduced me to the "wheel of fortune" technique,[3] another effective technique for visualizing and achieving greater Good in life. A wheel of fortune, as she calls it, is a large piece of poster board or cardboard on which you paste bright, colorful pictures of the Good you wish to manifest in your life. I've found that there are several ways of making a wheel of fortune.

The General Board: You can make one general, overall board or wheel that covers all the different areas of your life. You do this by dividing up the poster board or cardboard into four or five different areas, for example: 1) health, 2) prosperity, 3) family, 4) friends, 5) the spiritual quest. Look through books and magazines and find bright, happy pictures that illustrate the state of health, business success, family unity, etc., you wish to manifest in your life. Paste the different pictures in the area they belong to. In the middle of your board, write a positive affirmation or blessing dedicating your board to the Highest Good for yourself and all humanity.

The Specific Board: You can also make specific boards or wheels of fortune for the different areas of your life. For example, you can make an entire board about prosperity, or about love, or about health. Again follow the same principle as described above. Find bright, happy pictures that illustrate the positive outcome you are going to manifest.

Important Points

Keep it secret: When you make a wheel of fortune, don't show it to other people and don't talk about it. Keep your board hidden in a secret place. You don't need to convince others that what you believe is good and right for you. It's none of their business and you don't want their criticism or negative comments to neutralize your power.

Look at it every day: Look at your wheel every single day for a few minutes when you are alone.

Keep quiet about what you're doing. Do it every day.

Be careful: The power of visualization is immense, so choose your pictures with care. Don't forget you are picturing what you want to demonstrate in your life. Do not use pictures that are limiting, dark, or negative. Choose bright, bold, happy, colorful pictures for yourself. And don't clutter up your board with too many images either because it can be confusing.

Don't compromise: This is not an intellectual exercise, so you don't have to be logical about the Good you picture. Picture what you really want, not what other people want for you or what you think you should, could, or can have. Listen to the wisdom of your heart and picture what you really deeply and sincerely want to manifest in your life.

Colors: Use background paper of different colors for different subjects:

Green or gold for prosperity
White or yellow for spiritual growth and understanding
Orange or bright yellow for health and energy
Blue for intellectual achievement
Rose or pink for love and harmony

Bless your board: Dedicate your board to the Highest Good by placing a spiritual symbol or blessing on your board.

The wheel of fortune technique will help you visualize and mentally accept the new Good you want to bring forth in your life. As your new Good manifests and your life changes, you will naturally want to make new wheels of fortune to suit your new circumstances.

The Pocket Wheel of Fortune

If making a large wheel of fortune is difficult for you, or if you'd like to have something you can carry around with you during the day, you can make a secret little notebook for yourself. Follow the same technique as with the larger board. Paste bright, bold pictures in your book and write affirmations and blessings all around your pictures. Then when you have a free moment during the day, you can study your pictures to keep your mind positive and focused on visualizing your new Good.

Picture Good for Others

Not only can we visualize Good for ourselves, we can use our power to visualize Good for others too. Just take a moment and think about how you see, picture, visualize life for the troublesome people in your life.

If you have a sick relative, do you see him getting more and more ill? Do you see his darkened bedroom or antiseptic hospital room? Do you see more difficulty, more pain, and more suffering on his pathway? Or do you image him rapidly regaining his health? Every time you think of him, do you see him recovering, easily and effortlessly? Do you stubbornly refuse to pay his present illness any notice whatsoever? Do you picture him bright and cheerful, strong and healthy? Do you see the smile returning to his face and a song emanating from his lips?

Even if this is not the present situation, even if this is not true right now, you can call forth powerful, positive images of health and happiness for other people, just as you would do for yourself. So when you think of others, both near and far, why not use your power to visualize for their increased Good too? Our thoughts are always working on the vibrational level, influencing the people around us. This is why your positive images for others act as a kind of praise and blessing on the invisible level. (See Chapter 17 on The Power of Praise and Blessing.) Don't underestimate your power to bring forth the Good in every situation for other people too!

Mental Acceptance

As you continue to practice visualization, using the techniques described earlier, you will notice that you slowly but surely begin to *believe and accept* the pictures you have created for yourself and for others. You will notice that your belief and acceptance begin to feel natural and right, both emotionally and mentally. Then it's time to hold your hat, because when you reach this stage, amazing things start happening. . . .

Your pictures become your reality!

Congratulations!

You just won the lottery called the Game of Life!

Chapter 7

The Power of Alpha

Alpha is a great place to go—
it's better than Hawaii!

What is alpha?

Alpha is what we call the state we're in when our brain waves slow down to about half their normal frequency. This happens naturally just before we fall asleep and as we wake up in the morning. Researchers have found that good things happen to our bodies when our brains are at alpha level. Blood pressure becomes normal, pulse rate stabilizes, stressed, tense organs relax, and the body generally becomes revitalized.

This is the way scientists classify our brain waves: When we are active and wide awake, our brain waves pulsate at about 14–21 pulsations per second. This state is called beta. When we relax or are about to fall asleep, our brain waves slow down to 7–14 pulsations per second, to the state called alpha. As we enter sleep, pulsations slow down even more. Light sleep is called theta and is between 4–7 pulsations per second, and deep sleep or delta is anything fewer than 4 pulsations per second.

Beta:
  14–21 pulsations per second
  wide awake
  fully conscious

Alpha:
  7–14 pulsations per second
  deeply relaxed
  state of inner consciousness

Theta:
  4–7 pulsations per second
  light sleep
  state of inner consciousness

Delta:
  fewer than 4 pulsations per second
  deep sleep
  unconscious

The Place to Go
  So alpha is definitely a place to go. Why? Because alpha is a natural, comfortable, peaceful,

blissful, relaxed state. Everyone feels good when they're in alpha.

There are many different techniques for entering the alpha state, such as meditation, chanting, prayer, listening to soothing music, autogenic training, biofeedback, and so forth. Lots of people have their own special routines for or ways of sending themselves into alpha. In fact, many people are enjoying the alpha state when they're daydreaming . . . they just don't know they're in alpha. There are also many relaxation tapes that guide you easily and effortlessly into alpha.

Reprogram Yourself in Alpha

One of the interesting things about the alpha state is besides being a good place to release tension and stabilize body functions, you can reprogram yourself in alpha. This means that you can change your unconscious mental programs more easily because your subconscious mind is open and receptive when you are in alpha. Many people use the alpha state to cure themselves of health problems or initiate big and small changes in their behavior and in their lives. All this is possible in the receptive alpha state.

Creative Visualizations Work Better in Alpha

When you relax and enter the alpha state and visualize the new Good you want in your life, your visualizations manifest more quickly. (See Chapter 6 on The Power of Visualization.)

Alpha opens your subconscious mind which then accepts your visualizations without any interference from your intellect. This means that when you're in alpha, you don't have to explain to yourself *how* your new Good is going to come about. You don't have to be logical or try to understand how it will happen. All you have to do is visualize your Good, and then feel and believe your Good is manifesting, right here and now.

The Silva Mind Control Method

The Silva Mind Control Method is a simple, active way of learning to enter alpha and use the alpha state to achieve your goals, heal your body, relax your mind, and solve all sorts of problems.

Here is a basic technique for entering alpha from *You the Healer* by José Silva:

1. Sit comfortably in a chair and close your eyes.
2. Take a deep breath, and as you exhale, relax your body.

3. Count slowly backward from 100 to 1.
4. Daydream about some peaceful place you know.
5. Say to yourself mentally, *I will always maintain a perfectly healthy body and mind.*
6. Tell yourself mentally that when you open your eyes at the count of 5, you will feel wide awake and better than before. When you reach the count of 3, repeat this. When you open your eyes, affirm it again. Say, "I am wide awake and feeling better than before."[1]

There are many variations from Silva and others of this basic exercise for relaxing and entering alpha, and almost all of them work if practiced regularly.

If you are using the Silva Method, once you start to get good at relaxing, you don't need to continue to count backward from 100 to 1. After 10 days, you can shorten it to 50 to 1, after another 10 days count only from 25 to 1, and finally, when you become good at relaxing, it will be enough to count backward from 10 to 1.

Once you're in alpha, you can visualize healing all sorts of problems, from minor colds to more serious illnesses. You can also visualize the positive outcome of all types of situations, whether in the world of business or with people who trouble you.

Guided Meditation

Here is another easy way to relax and get into the alpha state:

Sit comfortably in a chair with your feet flat on the floor and your hands resting on your thighs— or lie on your back in bed with arms and legs outstretched, palms open and facing upward.

Now take a deep breath, hold it for a while, and then exhale . . . and as you do, feel yourself releasing all the tensions of the day.

Continue to breathe deeply and as you do, allow your attention to drift slowly to your forehead and scalp, neck and shoulders. Feel the tension flowing out of your forehead and scalp, feel your forehead and scalp relaxing. Now let the muscles around your eyes relax and as you do, continue to breathe deeply. Relax your lips and the muscles around your mouth. Let all the muscles in your face relax. Then feel your neck muscles relaxing, feel your whole neck relaxing.

Then move your attention down to your shoulders. Feel your shoulders relaxing. Just let the tension go and relax.

There is nothing to do, nothing to change, just let go and allow.

Now let the relaxation spread from your shoulders down to your back muscles, and feel the relaxation moving from your upper back to your lower back. Let yourself go deeper and deeper into a pleasant state of relaxation.

Let your chest muscles relax, and feel your heart beating calmly and easily. Relax your stomach and your abdominal muscles as you continue to breathe deeply and easily. Feel your pelvic muscles relax and feel the warm sensation of relaxation move down through your thighs, then into your knees, then down through your calves and finally into your feet and toes. Feel the warmth and relaxation all the way down in your toes.

Continue to breathe slowly and deeply and enjoy this state of total relaxation.

After a few minutes you can choose to count from 1 to 5 and wake yourself up, or you can now do a visualization exercise. (See Chapter 6 on The Power of Visualization.)

Always end by counting from 1 to 5. When you reach the count of 5 you will be wide awake and feeling much more relaxed and positive than before.

Create the Life You Want in Alpha
Once you learn how to reach alpha, you can start to use alpha to create the results you want in

your everyday life. It usually takes about thirty days to master the skill. Ten minutes of practice a day is enough to begin with.

For example, say you are going to an important business meeting or job interview. Before the event, take a few minutes to go into alpha and visualize the meeting or interview in as much detail as possible. Visualize the meeting going just the way you'd like it to proceed. See yourself relaxed and happy. See yourself presenting your points in a clear, friendly manner. Visualize the other people being open and receptive to you, and reacting in a positive manner to your presentation.

Visualize a positive outcome. Then count to 5, open your eyes, and affirm that you are wide awake and feeling fine. When you've finished the exercise, go about your normal daily activities. I guarantee you will be amazed at how often your meetings or interviews turn out exactly the way you visualized them in alpha.

Talk about a powerful tool!

Avoid Negative Influences When in Alpha

It makes sense that we instinctively feel we want to avoid negative situations or being with negative people when we are in a very relaxed state of mind. This is probably because we realize instinctively, even if we don't know exactly why, that we are much more open and receptive to every kind of influence when we are relaxed.

You could say there are different levels of people . . . those who bring you down and lower your energy, those who are on the same level as you are and whom you feel good with, and those who are on a higher level than you and who inspire you. When you are very relaxed, it's best to hang out with people who are on your own level or higher.

The Healing Power of Nature

Most people also instinctively love to be out in Nature when they want to slow down and relax. (See Chapter 14 on The Power of Nature.) That's because being in Nature can also send us naturally and effortlessly into the alpha state. In addition, the restful, healing green colors we see as we walk through the woods enhance our deep feeling of relaxation.

Chapter 8

The Power of Focus

Do you know what you want?

And how to get it?

Many people don't.

Not only do they not know what they want, if they knew, they wouldn't know how to get it either.

To know what you want—and get it too—is a matter of focus. In fact, the entire universe, as far as you and I are concerned, is a matter of focus.

What is focus?

Webster's Encyclopedic Unabridged Dictionary defines focus as: "the focal point . . . the clear and sharply defined condition of an image, the central point as of attraction, attention or activity . . . the ability to concentrate as *to focus one's thoughts. . . .*"[1]

Why do most people seem to have so much trouble focusing? Why is it so hard to concentrate one's thoughts on a chosen goal?

To be honest, I don't rightly know why, because everyone can focus.

Everyone Can Focus

In fact, focusing on a goal is the easiest thing in the world to do. Focusing just means to pay attention to, and to concentrate on, something. Actually, we're all experts at focusing because that's just what we're doing whenever we dwell on a subject.

Take hypochondriacs. Even though they don't usually produce what we would call "great results" in their lives, they in fact are experts at focusing. Unfortunately for them, they are using their innate powers of concentration to focus on everything that's wrong with them, instead of turning the x-ray beam of their minds to the single-minded pursuit of some higher goal. If hypochondriacs could only become so one-pointed when thinking about (dwelling on) getting well . . . .

To focus or become one-pointed in the positive sense of the word is a matter of choice. And wouldn't you rather be the one who's in control of your destiny, instead of letting your random thoughts control you? Because that's what happens when we use our power to focus in a negative fashion. Once you become aware of how your mind works, you can turn things around and train yourself to use your power of concentration to create and achieve what you want in your life.

So decide for yourself.

And realize that focusing is just a matter of conscious choice.

To focus means: You are going to bite your teeth into a situation, set your mind on a course, gird your loins for the journey no matter how long and arduous, and not let go until the universe delivers what you want.

If you grab it with your teeth and bite down hard, if you make up your mind that this piece of pie in the sky is *absolutely and positively* yours—right here, right now, right this minute—if you let it be known far and wide within your consciousness, if you demonstrate in thought and deed, that you're not going to let go until it happens . . . *it simply has to happen*. Because that's the way the universe works.

Realization on the inner plane =
demonstration on the outer plane

So I ask you now to let the full implication of this simple mechanism sink in. Allow yourself to understand it fully and to feel the joy of attainment that this truth implies. Because if you understand this mechanism correctly, you will realize that everything you want (whatever it is) is already yours.

And it's easy as pie.

The other thing is this: Don't waste a second of your time on doubt or worry. The less fuel you give to doubt and worry, the better. That's very important. Doubt and worry weaken your concentration and create crosscurrents in the energy you are putting out.

Think about it. . . . What is the true meaning of dedication? Dedication is a complete and total lack of doubt. Dedication is absolute devotion to your cause. Dedication is absolute faith that the universe has to deliver because this is the way the universe works.

As Deepak Chopra says in his book *Ageless Body, Timeless Mind*: "When you realize that you are held securely within this unchanging framework, the joy of free will arises. You cannot exercise free will if you fear that it will bring uncertainty, accidents, and calamity. To someone in unity, each choice is accepted within the overall pattern. If you choose A, the field will bend to accommodate you; if you choose B, the field will accommodate that, even if B is the exact opposite of A. All possibilities are acceptable to the field, since by definition the field is a state of possibilities."[2]

So understand how your mind works—and how the universe works—and *do not doubt*. Don't let the slightest flicker of uncertainty pass across the big screen in your head that we call your mind. Not even for a second. Instead, work yourself up into a white heat of belief. Back your focus, your one-pointedness with the emotional power of your belief. Commit wholly and earnestly to whatever it is, be it person or purpose, cause or goal. Be it money, marriage, or just a new pair of shoes. Then act accordingly and consider it done. . . .

> *Dedication*
> *is the warrior's prayer*
> *unto himself.*[3]
> STUART WILDE

Why does it work like this? Because this is the way the universe works. Nobody can explain *why*. But as I said at the beginning of this book, we human beings are starting to understand these mechanisms now, and a great shift in human consciousness is taking place. Einstein's theory of relativity, the new quantum physics, the realization that matter and energy are interchangeable, have triggered a growing awareness in many people that *we are what we think we are*. And that the universe responds to our thoughts, whatever they are. Consequently, we are continually becoming what we think we are becoming. Since the universe is always reflecting our thoughts back to us, we attract into our lives whatever we dwell upon, declare, decree, and focus on.

Or as Emmet Fox said, "Like attracts like."[4]

Or as I say, *You get what you think you're going to get.*

To Find Your Goal, Release the Old

Sounds great, you say, but what if I don't know what I want to focus on. Obviously it's difficult to use your power to concentrate or focus to achieve your heart's desire if you don't know what your heart's desire is.

One good way to find out what you really want is to let go of or release what you don't want. (See Chapter 4 on The Power of Release.)

In other words, you've asked yourself: What is the mission of my life? What is my dream? What is the divine plan for my stay on Earth? And you've come up with absolute zilch.

If that's the case, if you really don't know what you want to do, achieve, be, or become, you can start cleaning up your act and creating clarity in your life by letting go of everything you are absolutely sure you don't want.

Release and let go of possessions, places, situations, people, circumstances, and relationships that no longer interest you. Just bless them with love and let them go. Create some empty space around yourself. Let some fresh air into your room, house, relationships, and life. I guarantee that interesting things will begin to happen.

Make Lists

Making lists is a very good way to clarify things for yourself. List making will help you find out what you really want. And list making is a good way to start focusing on your goals.

For starters, I suggest using The Three List Technique, described below. It's really quite simple, but before you start, let me remind you that you are not doing this exercise for anybody else. You are doing this exercise for *you*. Nobody else is going to read what you write, so be honest with yourself. And when you start writing, don't forget that you can always change your mind. This is an ongoing process of growth. If you write something today that you disagree with tomorrow, just change it. You can make as many lists as you like. You can rewrite them, redo them, refashion them, throw them all out, and start over every single day of the week if you want to. (This isn't a bad idea if you feel confused about your true goals.)

This exercise is meant for you. This exercise is

just practice. It's strictly for your eyes only, so keep your lists secret!

The Three List Technique

1) Your Letting Go List:
   Start by making a list of everything you are sure you don't want in your life. List items, people, mental conditions and attitudes, emotions, relationships, and situations at work. Don't be wishy-washy about things. Don't think about what other people might think about your Letting Go List. Just write down whatever you'd like to get rid of or release from your life. List everything that you feel is no longer for your Highest Good. It doesn't matter if the person or thing was once very important to you. Remember, releasing doesn't mean you don't like somebody or are condemning anything. Something that once served you well can have outlived its usefulness to you. So bless it with love and let it go.

   At the end of your Letting Go List, write an affirmation of release or blessing. Write something like this: I now fully and freely release all of this from my life. I bless these people and situations with love and let them go. I relax, release, and let you all go to your Highest Good.

2) Your Wishing List:
   Here you should write down everything you think you would like to demonstrate in your life. Don't be afraid to list *everything* you want, your every desire. Don't write down what you think other people think you should have. Don't write down what you think other people would think is okay or acceptable for you to have or to be. This list is supposed to be what you really would like to manifest in your life. Are you sure this is all you want? Don't you want more? Don't worry about how your heart's desire compares to what you think other people want. What other people want is their business. What you want is your choice because this is your life. So don't worry about writing down things which seem totally "crazy" or hard to achieve at the moment. If you want them, write them down. As I said, this is a private list, for your own enlightenment only. This list is meant to give you something to work with, to help you focus and grow. Imagine you are a sculptor molding a piece of clay that is going to be your

life. And don't forget you're not going to show this work of art (your list) to anyone. This is your secret playground. Then ask yourself: What is the real reason you're not writing down everything you really want? Is it because you're afraid you don't deserve what you really and truly want?

Write an affirmation at the end of your list, something like this: I bless my desires with divine love and know that the universe now manifests that which is for my Highest Good. The Good of one is the Good of all.

3) Your Appreciation List:
Finally, to put all this list making into perspective and help you realize how well your life is already working, I suggest you finish this exercise by making a list of all the things in your life you feel thankful for. In other words, a list of how much the universe has already given you, the abundance that is already yours. This is an interesting exercise because once you get started, you'll find your appreciation list just keeps on growing. Just looking at this list is a sure way to make yourself feel better and happier than you did before you started. And the act of giving thanks and feeling deep appreciation has

the magical power to open your heart and attract more Good into your life.

How Napoleon Hill Helped Me

When I found myself alone, a single parent with three small children to support, Napoleon Hill helped me. At the time, I had no money and no obvious way to make money. Still, I had a strong feeling that it didn't have to be that way. I felt I had the talent and ability to make money. My big problem was I didn't quite know how to proceed. I needed a concrete tool or plan to show me what practical steps to take to gain control of my life and financial affairs. I found them in one of the original, classic self-help books: *Think and Grow Rich* by Napoleon Hill.

Inspired by the rags-to-riches story of the great American multimillionaire Andrew Carnegie, Hill devoted his life to studying successful people in order to uncover the secrets behind their amazing achievements. How did these people move from often extremely humble origins and/or difficult circumstances to demonstrate such enormous success and wealth?

Think and Grow Rich presents many of their secrets and techniques, including the role of desire, faith, persistence, planning, organizing, and such mind techniques as auto-suggestion or visualization, Master Mind groups (see Chapter 18 on The Power of Friends), and more.

Hill says in his book: "Every human being who reaches the age of understanding of the purpose of money wishes for it. *Wishing* will not bring riches. But *desiring* riches with a state of mind that becomes an obsession, then planning definite ways and means to acquire riches, and backing those plans with persistence which *does not recognize failure*, will bring riches."[5]

Here I quote in full the Napoleon Hill exercise that got me started:

Six Ways to Turn Desires into Gold
The method by which *desire* for riches can be transmuted into its financial equivalent, consists of six definite, practical steps, viz:

First: fix in your mind the *exact* amount of money you desire. It is not sufficient merely to say "I want plenty of money." Be definite as to the amount.

Second: determine exactly what you intend to *give* in return for the money you desire. (There is no such reality as "something for nothing.")

Third: establish a definite date when you intend to *possess* the money you desire.

Fourth: create a definite plan for carrying out your desire, and begin *at once,* whether you are ready or not, to put this plan into *action.*

Fifth: write out a clear, concise statement of the amount of money you intend to acquire, name the time limit for its acquisition, state what you intend to give in return for the money, and describe clearly the plan through which you intend to accumulate it.

Sixth: read your written statement aloud, twice daily, once just before retiring at night, and once after arising in the morning. As you read—see and feel and believe yourself already in possession of the money.[6]

I used Hill's exercise with great success for many years. From my humble starting point, I sat down and decided each year exactly how much money I wanted to make. Then I decided exactly what I was going to give in exchange for that amount of money. I then made a written statement as described above, mounted it on a piece of cardboard, and placed it by my bed. I read my statement aloud first thing every morning and last thing every evening before I went to sleep. I then closed my eyes, relaxed, and visualized my desired results in as much detail as possible. I saw myself doing the work I planned to do and receiving the fair payment I described for myself. I imagined having the money in my hands and putting it into my bank account.

Interestingly enough, every year I made *exactly* the amount of money I said I was going to make. Then every year I rewrote my statement, raised my goal, reevaluated what I was going to give in exchange for the money, and continued. And every year I reached my goal.

> *Whatever the mind of man*
> *can conceive and believe*
> *it can achieve.*[7]
> NAPOLEON HILL

When in Doubt, Withdraw

Once you start learning to focus and using your power of concentration to achieve your goals, you will find that your power or ability varies. You will experience days, weeks, or months when your ability to focus is strong and powerful. Then suddenly, for reasons you may or may not understand, you will feel your forces are scattered and you've lost your ability to concentrate or focus.

When this happens, when you lose your focus and don't feel "right" or "strong," when you feel you've suddenly lost your sense of direction, it's always best to stop and withdraw for a while. If it's within your power, just stop and wait.

In other words, do nothing. Nothing is definitely the best cure for a sudden loss of focus. In the nothingness, in the silence, in the probably much needed moment of no significance, your focus and power will come back to you. (See Chapter 13 on The Power of Silence.)

This is because we are all so "outer" directed. When we're busy, we have a tendency to forget how the universe works. We think it's the world "out" there that is influencing us, when in fact it's not really out there at all. It's the world "in" here, inside us, that is the source of everything that's happening out there.

So remember that—and retreat, shut down, look inward when things seem diffuse, scattered, or difficult out there.

That, in fact, is what your loss of focus is telling you. It's screaming to you: Step back, step down, step aside! Get out of the way, move out of the center of attention, leave the playing field for a while, go take a cold shower, go into hiding, and look within. Find out what's going on inside of you, find out what's out of sync in your mind and/or body. Find out what you're saying, thinking, doing that's not in harmony with your purpose or goal. Find out why you're resisting. Get yourself straightened out.

And if you can, don't go out there again until your focus returns. You won't be in doubt when you are ready and able to focus again.

Ways to Practice Focusing

There are so many ways to practice focusing. I discuss other techniques in the chapters on The Power of Affirmation, The Power of Visualization, The Power of Praise and Blessing, and The Power of Silence. In fact, you could say this whole book is about focusing techniques. So for fast results, pick the techniques that are closest to your heart and get started!

Chapter 9

The Power of Secrecy

Don't give away your power by telling other people your plans, dreams, hopes, prayers, visualizations, or affirmations. And don't show other people your wheels of fortune, treasure maps, or lists.

All these techniques to gain power are for you alone.

When you reveal, share, or show, you dissipate your energy. This is because you are working on the invisible plane, on the vibrational level, where divine substance or the quantum soup is being formed, through your mind, into your reality.

Your inner work has nothing to do with other people.

Your inner work is your task.

Your inner work is your challenge.

Your inner work is yours alone.

When you speak of your dreams and plans to others, their input, comments, criticism, suggestions (no matter how loving) will rob you of your power.

So keep your plans, visualizations, notes, lists, and affirmations secret.

Talking too much about anything, not just your plans, dissipates your power too.

So keep your mouth shut as much as possible.

Keep your focus.

Actually it's much easier to stay focused when your mouth is shut.

Also, if you're confused, try to stop talking. Just keep quiet.

If you're very confused, try not to talk for a whole day and see what happens. (See Chapter 13 on The Power of Silence.) You'll be surprised how silence clears the mind.

Chapter 10

The Power of Money

Most people I talk to have negative programs about money. If you take time to notice, people are always talking about money. And without being aware of it, they quickly reveal their beliefs about money and prosperity.

Most people believe in lack.

Many people believe they'll never be prosperous.

And many even believe they don't deserve to be prosperous.

Did you learn ideas like these when you were growing up? Money doesn't grow on trees. Money is the root of all evil.

If you did, do they improve the quality of your life? Do they make you happy, healthy, and prosperous?

I have noticed that it is often harder to talk to people about money, about their relationship to money, about their beliefs about money, than it is to talk about their sex lives or other so-called "personal" matters like their health or their relationship with their husbands or wives.

What Is Money?

Money is just a symbol, a symbol of energy. Money, you could say, represents the substance (matter) of our universe.

Einstein's theory of relativity demonstrated the interchangeability of substance (matter) and energy. Scientists also tell us that there is an infinite supply of substance (matter) and energy and that there is no limit to or lack of substance or energy in this universe. If this is true, why should we lack?

Poverty Causes Misery

Money is not the source of misery, violence, crime, revolution, drug addiction, or unhappiness—poverty is. If you look closely at the stories behind the bad news, you will find that poverty is almost always behind violence, crime, misery, drug addiction, and unhappiness between people. I think it's pretty easy to conclude that:

Poverty is no fun.
It's hard to be happy if you are poor.
Financial problems and pressures are terribly stressful.

Financial problems and pressures often cause nervous breakdowns.

Poverty can drive people to drink and drugs.

Poverty is not only uncomfortable, it is a degrading experience.

Nobody really wants to be poor.

Normal, healthy people want to have enough money to enjoy the good things in life.

If you're honest with yourself, you'll have to admit that this is true. We all have a deep desire to enjoy the blessings and abundance of this infinite universe even though most of us have been brought up to believe that wealth is sinful. But if you recognize that we live in an abundant universe, why shouldn't we enjoy all the Good the universe has for us?

Attitudes Toward Money

Since our attitudes govern our lives, our attitudes toward money determine whether we live a life of lack or one of increasing prosperity. Do you bless your money? Do you give thanks for the blessings you already have? Do you feel you deserve abundance? If not, why not? Do you believe there is more than enough for everyone?

Focus on Prosperity

Focus on prosperity and your income will increase. Since we always manifest what we focus on, when we focus on abundance, when we feel we deserve abundance, when we joyfully accept and praise the money we have right now, we automatically attract more money.

> *The Law of Mind says:*
> *Like attracts like.*[1]
> EMMET FOX

Most people are using the law of attraction to do the opposite—to stay poor. Without being aware of it, they focus on and create lack in their lives by complaining about their lack of money, the high level of taxes, the high cost of living, the government, the high level of unemployment, and so forth.

Change Your Money Program

If you want to change your life, stop talking about lack. Refuse to listen to people who complain about lack. Don't participate in conversations about lack. And don't think negative thoughts about your financial situation, about the money in your bank account, or about your debts.

Instead of resenting your debts, try this. Regard

every bill that drops into your mailbox as a sign that someone trusted you. They trusted you enough and believed enough in your ability to pay for these goods and services to actually give you the stuff in advance, way before you paid for it! What faith! Actually, you should bless all these bills because they are a symbol of your ability to pay for whatever you now have in your life!

Clean Up Your Act

So it's very simple. Since your money is a symbol of the abundance of the universe, it's very important to clean up your mental act in relation to money.

Don't limit yourself to a "fixed income" either. Remember, we live in an infinite universe, so abundance can come to you from many sources. Be open to new channels of supply. Be aware that your Good can come from expected and unexpected sources. Affirm daily that your Good is increasing and that it's on its way to you now. Affirm daily that you are open and receptive to a major increase in your level of prosperity right here and right now. Say yes to new Good in your life.

For example, decree for yourself:

I am open and receptive to increasing prosperity.

The universe now richly provides.

New financial channels are now opening up for me.

_____ (state the specific amount of money) comes to me now. And I accept it gladly.

Abundant supply now floods my bank account. I am open to a great increase in my financial income and give thanks for this plentiful increase now.

I give thanks for ever-increasing prosperity now. As I bless and praise my wealth, it grows.

Visualize Prosperity

You can use your power to visualize to increase your income too. Since the thoughts and mental images we consistently hold in our minds are the blueprints for life we place in our subconscious minds, whatever we picture or visualize on a consistent basis will become our reality. One of the ways to create abundance in your life is to visualize abundance on a daily basis. (For more about visualization techniques, see Chapter 6 on The Power of Visualization.)

Relax as described in Chapter 7 on The Power of Alpha, and then visualize or see with as many details as possible the prosperity you desire.

Let's take an example. Let's say you are a real estate agent and you want to sell three houses this month. For the sale of these three houses, you are going to earn _____ (state the exact amount of money) in commission. Visualize yourself in the present tense (*right now*) successfully selling each one of these houses. Picture each house in detail, picture the people who are going to buy it, picture the exact time of the day when you are selling the house. Picture how the people look. Imagine the pleasure they feel in finding the house of their dreams. See yourself driving them back to your office and watching them sign the papers. Imagine the exact sum of money each house is being sold for. Imagine the exact amount of your commission. See yourself collecting the money and depositing the check in your bank account. Feel the pleasure of having _____ (state exact amount) now in your bank account. Just enjoy the feeling. Then imagine how you are going to spend this money: the improvements you'll make in your life, what you will buy, where you will go, etc.

Not Too Modest or Too Wild

When doing this type of visualization exercise, it's important that you visualize what is right for you. Your pictures should not be too modest, but not too wild either in relation to your present situation. You must feel congruent or compatible with your visualizations. In other words, you must be able to mentally accept and emotionally feel good with your pictures and images, with the amount of money, and with the situations you are visualizing.

For best results, repeat this visualization exercise every day for thirty days in a row. When you are first learning this technique, it's best to stick to the same goal and keep visualizing the same result for a while. As you get more advanced and begin to see results manifesting in your life, you will be able to change your pictures more often to fit your changing needs and the different situations you find yourself in.

Act Prosperously

Once you begin to release your negative attitudes toward abundance and start changing the way you think about money, e.g. by visualizing a major leap in prosperity in your life, it's time to begin acting prosperously too.

By this I mean, if the universe is abundant, it's time to focus on the abundance you already have in your life. Don't forget, what you focus on grows. (See Chapter 8 on The Power of Focus.) So act prosperously. Wear your best clothes when you go shopping or to meetings instead of saving

them for the future, even if you don't o‍
expensive clothes.

It's important not to wait for tomorrow to enjoy
the riches you already have. By enjoying feeling
prosperous now, by putting your best foot for-
ward, you attract more prosperity into your life.

It's also a good idea to enjoy the wealth you see
around you, whether it is yours or not. You might
want to walk through expensive shops or restau-
rants just to "feel" the ambiance of money. If you
are going to visualize an increase in income for
yourself, you must feel "comfortable" in more
prosperous surroundings. Realize that the fact
that other people are wealthy is just a sign that
there is an abundance of wealth in the universe.
You should be delighted to know that if other people can manifest prosperity in their lives, you can
too.

Don't envy other people's wealth because
when you feel envious, you are really affirming
lack. Your envy is a sign that you don't really believe that you deserve abundance or that there is
wealth enough for you.

Are You Shocked?

Many people find these new attitudes to abundance, wealth, prosperity, and money shocking
when they first hear them. Often this is because

most of us have been brought up to believe there is something sinful about money. On closer inspection, most people are relieved when they truly understand that since we live in an infinite universe, abundance is our birthright. This also means that there is more than enough for everyone, which is important because no one wants to feel that their prosperity or gain is someone else's loss.

In the end, we realize that what we truly want is abundance and prosperity for all people on Earth. And that the only sinful thing about money is the lack of it and the poverty-consciousness that so many people are demonstrating in their daily lives at the moment.

Chapter 11

The Power of Giving

Everything in the universe is in a state of constant flux. Nothing is static; nothing remains the same forever. In fact, the only thing that never changes is change itself.

Even though we might like to think of ourselves as solid, stable, and permanent, it's only our small egos strutting about when we talk or think like this. In fact, our skin, bones, stomachs, hearts, lungs, and brains are constantly disappearing into thin air to be replaced by new atoms and new cells as fast as they vanish. Our skin renews itself every month, we build a new stomach lining every five days, our liver is renewed every six weeks, and even our seemingly solid skeleton is in fact completely replaced every three months. During the course of one year, 98 percent of the atoms in our bodies are exchanged for new ones.

Yet despite this constant flux, we are eternal beings in a sea of constant change. We are symphonies of light who incarnate in bodies made up of minute, fast-moving particles of energy. There's nothing solid about us, our surroundings, or our planet.

Everything is in a state of constant flux.

Everything is changing.

And anything that resists this constant change causes problems.

All sickness
is basically congestion.

All healing
is basically circulation.

Giving Is Circulation

This is why it's so important to give. Giving is circulation, the universal cure-all. Not for the sake of others, but for our own sake.

Giving is an affirmation, a way of declaring that we understand the nature of the universe.

Give and you will receive.

Give Your Way to Health, Wealth, and Happiness

People who amass, accumulate, collect, or hoard things they don't need, people who are stingy, people who are afraid of spending their money or who hide their money away in vaults and secret bank accounts, people who are possessive about their children, friends, or loved ones, are all resisting the natural order of the universe, which is *constant flow and change.*

Since we live in the midst of this massive flow of energy, since we're all just channels through which the energy flows, we can only be fine, okay, healthy, happy, prosperous, productive, and enjoy life when we give and receive naturally. When we don't think about giving and receiving, but just do it, when we give naturally because this is the nature of life, of being okay, then we are in harmony with the universe. Circulation is the natural order of things.

In fact, when you think about it, everything is already given to us: life, air, water, our parents, our bodies, food, this planet, and people to play with. So why should we try to hold on to anything . . . when we already have everything? Why should we resist the flow? Of course, when we do, it's because of fear. Fear that we will lose something, fear that we won't have enough. But this fear is just an illusion. This fear springs from a basic lack of understanding of the nature of the universe. Once you remember your true origin, once you realize you already have everything, you can dissolve this fear.

So if you have any problem in your life and you want to feel better: Start giving right away! Especially when things in your life seem stuck, or when you're sick, or when you seem to lack financial means—that's when it's time to give. Giving opens up the channels again. Giving gets rid of congestion. Giving keeps the energy circulating, flowing. Giving will open the doors again so you can receive because *you must give in order to receive* . . . just as in Nature you must sow before you can harvest. This is the universal law. When you do not give or sow, you cannot reap.

There Are Many Ways to Give

Giving is an act of faith. Giving says you recognize that the infinite universe is the true source of all life, all abundance, and that you are a worthy child of this infinite universe who expects to receive all the blessings and abundance that the universe provides.

You can give:

Time
Money
Possessions
Praise and blessings
Love
Understanding

And you can give to:

Spiritual or religious organizations
People who give you spiritual inspiration and guidance
Organizations that work for peace or the environment
Charity, humanitarian, or cultural organizations
Other people
Yourself

Tithing

Tithing is the ancient religious practice of giving a tenth of your income to the religious and/or spiritual group, organization, or church that is providing you with spiritual inspiration and guidance. Tithing is a time-honored system and symbol of trust or faith in the God Force or Infinite Universe that provides us with all things. By giving a tenth of our income back to the source, we open the channels to receive from the source. We remove the blockages; we get things circulating again.

The mysterious prospering power of tithing is legendary. Numerous spiritual books speak of the importance of tithing. If you delve into the lives of great people and famous millionaires, you will discover that many were and are consistent tithers.

I also recommend tithing as a way of establishing spiritual calm and equilibrium in your life. When you tithe, you will feel a new sense of peacefulness. You will feel connected to the greater source of all life, and new blessings and new Good will miraculously appear in your life.

I also recommend that you keep your tithing secret. It is no one's business but your own. You are tithing for your own Highest Good and no one needs to know. (See Chapter 9 on The Power of Secrecy.) Also remember to keep your focus and tithe regularly (for example, every month) and consistently to the same spiritual teacher or organization, with no strings attached as to how the money is to be used. Then trust in the universe. Trust in life. Let things circulate. Then expect the highest and best to manifest in your life.

Chapter 12

The Power of Love

The Wise forever proclaim that Love is the greatest power in the Universe, the Ultimate Truth, the Divine Light. I believe it's true and you probably do too. If we believe this is true . . . are our lives a demonstration of this belief?

Anger Doesn't Work

We've all tried anger, and many of us are slowly learning that anger just doesn't work. Oh yes, anger might seem to work in the short run, but don't let it fool you, it's just an illusion, a short-term solution.

This is because anger, like its close relative violence, is always trying to *force* other people to do what we want them to do or what we think is best for them. If a solution is arrived at through anger or violence, you can be sure it is not for everyone's Highest Good, so it won't last. In the long run, it will crumble, fade, and disappear.

As far as I can see, you probably won't be able

to give up anger as a problem-solving method until you realize that nobody, and I mean nobody, is going to come and *save you from your life*. You are going to have to do it all by yourself. And when you realize that the responsibility for your life is yours and yours alone, love becomes a serious option.

People Problems

Most of our problems in life are people problems. Just think about it for a moment. Don't most of your problems revolve around other people? Isn't it usually the people at work, or your in-laws, or your friends, or the authorities, or the other people on your street or in your neighborhood?

At the workplace, I seldom see people having serious problems with their jobs because they are bumbling idiots who don't have the skill to do the job at hand. Nine times out of ten, it's because they don't know how to get along with other people. Their problems are people problems because they're either too impatient, too unpleasant, too inconsiderate, too sloppy, or too angry to get along with others. In short, getting along with others is the key issue, not the job at hand.

The only viable solution is the problem-solving power of love.

Now by this, I don't mean mushy, sentimental, emotional, romantic, or melodramatic love.

I mean impersonal love or love without attachment, the kind of love that is eternal, infinite, and divine, the love that holds our universe together and that translates into the Highest Good for everyone involved in every situation.

You can only feel this kind of love, love without sentimental or emotional attachment, when you realize that everyone on the planet is going through the learning experiences he or she needs to further their soul development and growth. When we recognize this, we also realize it's none of our business, nor is it our job or mission, to interfere or infringe on other people's evolutionary experiences. This kind of non-attached love is all-encompassing or universal. This kind of love lets other people grow and evolve in whatever ways are best for them.

Bless Them with Love

Whenever you have problems with other people, whether at home or at work, that is the time to bless both the people and the problems with love. Of course it's nice and it's easier to bless the people you love and care for, and of course you should bless them. Obviously it's much harder to bless the people who bother you, but it should help you to know that blessing difficult, irritating people with love really works wonders too.

For example, if you are having a problem with someone at your office, try to visualize the person and the situation surrounded by the white light of divine love. (See Chapter 6 on The Power of Visualization.) Sit quietly for a few minutes and see the problem with this person being solved in a harmonious, loving manner. Surround this troublesome person/situation with love. Then bless the person/situation with love and decree aloud if you are alone: "I bless you _____ (name) with love."

You can also say the same for the situation. For example, "I bless the matter of _____ at the office with love."

Say your affirmations aloud fifteen times in a row. (See Chapter 3 on The Power of Affirmation.)

I also find that amazing things happen when I'm in an unpleasant situation if I silently bless the people involved with love. It's as if everything changes when loving vibrations enter the situation.

> Bless a thing and it will bless you.
> Curse a thing and it will curse you.[1]
> EMMET FOX

Bless Everything
Not only can you bless difficult people and situations with love, you can bless everything in

your life with love, from your car to your computer and washing machine to your local grocer and your monthly bills. As you do, you will notice how things begin to flow more easily for you. Life changes when you stop resisting and fighting. When you no longer curse something, but bless it with love instead, its behavior changes, even if it is a so-called inanimate object like your computer. This is, after all, an intelligent universe we live in.

Bless your life, your body, your health, your work, your problems, your food, your home, your past, your present, your childhood, your future, your teachers, your books, your music, your possessions, your tools, your friends, your enemies, your family, your partner, your children, your parents, your job, your colleagues, your car, your money, your income, your debts, your bills, your street, your neighborhood, your country, the planet, the sun, the moon, the stars, the universe. . . . Surround and bless everything with love.

How My Son Blessed the Clinic

My son was going to a special clinic for some problem he had with his feet. One day he came home from the clinic and complained that the place was more like a factory than a place of healing. He said you had to wait such a long time until it was your turn, and when finally it was your turn, the doctors didn't even have enough time to speak civilly to their patients or explain what they were doing.

I suggested that the next time he was scheduled to go, he try blessing both the doctors and the clinic with love before he went and that he visualize the clinic and the treatment the way he thought it should be. I also suggested that he bless the doctors and nurses while he was there and try to think about how these people were dedicating their lives to helping other people and how thankful we should be for their skills and service.

After his next visit, he came home and told me: "It was amazing. First of all, I didn't have to wait at all when I got there. And as I continued blessing the doctors and nurses, they were all so nice to me. Everyone smiled and was so friendly. And this time the doctor had plenty of time to explain to me in detail what he was doing and how many times he thought I would have to come back for more treatments."

Love requires no practice. Love is.
One cannot practice is-ness.
One can, however, practice the decision to love.[2]
EMMANUEL

chapter 13

The Power of Silence

Silence is food for the soul, a gift from God. Without silence, we may wither, become confused, or fail to realize our full potential.

Silence is a wonderful place where wonderful things happen. . . . Silence is where we get in touch with our inner voice, our intuition, our deepest feelings, dreams, and desires. . . . Silence is where we find the answers to questions that trouble us and the solutions to problems that seem insoluble.

So don't be afraid of silence. Seek it out. Because silence is your friend. Silence is a true blessing.

Unfortunately, many people fear silence because they do not realize that silence is their friend. A place of power, a magic garden, a sacred haven, where they can regroup, recharge, and revitalize their energy. So they only feel comfortable when they are surrounded by incessant activity, noise, talk, music, television, and the frantic pace of city life. When such people are not working, they're talking on the phone, making plans, watching television, meeting friends, going out, doing things. They're always busy and have forgotten the importance of maintaining a harmonious balance between activity and rest.

Often there is the mistaken idea that something is wrong with us if we're not doing something all the time. Are you like this? Do you believe you've got to be "productive," "active" all the time? If this is your program, I suggest you do yourself a big favor and let this idea go, because not only are you missing one of life's true pleasures, you are missing a God-given place of power. So please be clear about this: You are dissipating your life force and your creative energy if you never take time to renew yourself through silence.

Do you fear silence?
To fear silence is to fear yourself.

10 Minutes of Silence Daily

Try stopping, once a day, every day, in the middle of your busyness and activities, and take ten minutes to practice silence. You can do this at the office or at home. All you have to do is decide to do it.

Just sit still and be quiet. Don't do anything

else. Allow yourself to settle down without thinking about anything special. For those few minutes, close your door and take the phone off the hook. Create an oasis of peace and quiet for yourself, and don't dwell on anything in particular. Let your mind go where it wants to go.

After ten minutes, return to your life. You will be amazed at the difference, especially if you practice short periods of silence on a daily basis. You will find that your ability to concentrate on the tasks at hand will increase. You will accomplish more with less effort.

An Afternoon or Day of Silence

One of the best treats you can give yourself is an afternoon or a day of silence. Especially out in Nature. As your soul absorbs the quietness of Nature and unwinds from the busyness of your everyday life, you might find yourself feeling like a junkie suffering from withdrawal symptoms. It's not always pleasant at first, but eventually you will find yourself calming down. After a while, the chatter in your brain will ebb and you will begin to breathe more deeply.

Without thinking, without questioning, the silence will begin to unfold, like a precious treasure, and reveal its secrets. It will bring you startling insights and guide you, showing you the way in matters that have confused you. And more than anything, the silence will bring you an abundance of new life, new energy, and new creative ideas.

Don't be dismayed if the silence does not reveal its secret treasures to you on your first try. Your soul may be so used to incessant activity and chatter that it will take a while to adjust to silence. But as long as you practice silence on a regular basis, even for short periods, it will eventually open its doors to you because silence is our direct link to the God Force or Higher Intelligence that underlies and guides the universe. Silence is always available to you, always waiting to bring you solace, power, and guidance.

Creativity and Silence: Learning to Await the Small Voice Within

Silence always precedes creative endeavor.

If you watch carefully, you will discover that it's the quiet time, the empty space, before the act of creativity that gives birth to all creative endeavor and human achievement.

It's as if all thoughts and things emerge from the silence to grow and take form in our minds, first as ideas, and later as all the wondrous creations of humanity.

Sometimes the most difficult part of the creative process is that period of silence that precedes activity. This is because we often struggle unnecessarily and try to force results instead of resting in the silence and awaiting the small voice within. . . .

Chapter 14

The Power of Nature

One of the reasons we feel so much better when we are out in Nature is that we are so much closer to the Force. Sometimes we even feel we're in direct contact. Then it's the most wonderful, electrifying sensation. . . . We feel strong, high, connected. We feel the Force pulsing through everything; we feel the flow and strength of it, moving in us and through us. Obviously it's much easier to feel this power outdoors, out in the woods or up in the mountains, because there's no noise, no town, no phones, no TVs, no egos, no rush, no violence, no cars, no man-made things or emotions to divert our attention and/or clutter our consciousness.

Outdoors, if we slow down and are quiet for just a little while—then wham bang—we become aware of the universal presence. We know the Force is right there, with us and in us!

Keep Quiet

Of course it's fun to go walking in the woods with our friends and of course we should do it. But not all the time because when we're with friends, we tend to talk and gossip and yak the whole time. When this happens, when we bring all our emotions and incessant chatter with us to the great outdoors, it's hard for the Force to get our attention, because the Force doesn't sing or dance. The Force is just there. Timeless and always present, just beneath the surface. So we have to be silent enough, and open and receptive enough, for it to do its wonderful work in us. (See Chapter 13 on The Power of Silence.)

Power Spots

There are places out there, places on this earth, that are more powerful than others. If you've ever been to a power spot, you know what I mean. A power spot overwhelms you with its clarity and beauty, with its sense of harmony, and with the feeling of power you experience when you stand on that spot. Some spots on the planet are so powerful that they work their magic for everybody. The desert around Santa Fe has this feeling and there are places in Denmark which do too.

But since we're all different, we can all have our special power spots too. I go to my power spots when I am in need of healing or to recharge and renew myself. For me, these places are truly sacred ground. As soon as I approach one of my special spots, I always feel much better. Just the memory of past harmony and healing instantly triggers a deep sense of peace and healing in my soul.

Find Your Own Power Spot

If you don't already have your own power spot, I suggest you make up your mind to find a spot that is right for you. A place in Nature that gives you this sense of power and harmony and where you can renew yourself. If you don't know how or where to begin, follow your intuition and just let your feet take you away.

Be open and receptive to the small voice within. Then, in your silent wandering, you will know when you find such a spot because you will feel so much better—healed of whatever ails you—after resting, relaxing, meditating, or just doing nothing on a natural power spot.

Move in Nature

Besides being silent, resting, relaxing, and quietly tuning in to the power of Nature, we can also increase our power by releasing, moving, exercising, singing, and dancing outdoors.

If something is bothering you, you can try, for

example, to release the situation and your emotions about the situation when you're alone out in the woods. Find a quiet spot or pathway and say affirmations of release aloud to the trees and the winding pathways until you feel a sense of peace. (See Chapter 3 on The Power of Affirmation.)

Say aloud, for example:

I now fully and freely release _____ (the person or situation). I bless you, _____ (person, situation), and let you go from my life. All disharmony between us is now dissolved. You are completely free to go on to your Highest Good and I am completely free to go on to my Highest Good. All things are in perfect harmony between us, now and forever.

Find or create an affirmation that feels right to you and fits your problem or situation. Keep repeating your affirmation until you feel peaceful. When you feel a deep sense of peace and quiet inside, you will know your work is done. Then forget the whole matter and enjoy your forest walk!

Hug a Tree

Tree hugging is also a good grounding exercise when you're out in Nature. I have my special trees that I like to hug and when I do, I always feel better. I embrace my tree with both arms and hug away, with my feet firmly planted on the ground next to the tree's trunk. I enjoy feeling the enormous energy of the tree. As I hug away, I let myself follow the energy as it flows up from the tree's massive roots buried deep down in the ground and surges upward through the branches, reaching for the sky.

It's also good to stand with your back against the trunk of a tree and feel its energy running up and down your spine. This is a good exercise when things are stuck or stagnated in your life because it helps get your energy flowing.

See the Aura

If you want to practice seeing auras or the energy fields that surround every living thing, a tree is a good place to start. It's easy to see a tree's aura.

Pick a nice big tree, one that you intuitively know is bursting with energy. Stand a good distance from the tree so you can see the whole tree. Take a few deep breaths and relax. Look at the top of the tree, at the twelve o'clock position and notice the blue sky that surrounds the tree itself. Now move your eyes so you are looking at the one o'clock position above the tree. Then relax and let your eyes go out of focus. Now, without trying to refocus, look back out of the corner of your eyes to the twelve o'clock position. You will see that the tree is surrounded by a whitish-bluish-grayish border. This is the tree's field of energy or aura. As you get a little better at doing this, you will be able to see the aura around the whole tree. (It's best not to stand so you are looking directly into the sun.) Keep practicing and you'll find you have a natural talent for seeing auras! We all do. Then try seeing the auras of plants, flowers, animals, and people.

chapter 15

The Power of Eating Less

There is only one way to eat less. *Stop thinking about food.*

Most people want to eat less because they want to lose weight. Of course, being nice and thin looks good, but that's not why I bring it up here.

There's more to eating less than being skinny.

The real point is this: *If you eat less, you gain power.*

First of all, when you eat less, you think more clearly.

And second, you have more energy.

And third, when you eat less it's a whole lot easier to focus. Unless, of course, you're starving hungry all the time, but that's not what I mean by eating less.

By eating less, I mean eating less than you think you need. Most people eat much more than they need to eat and many are indulging in wild orgies of food overkill.

Not only does eating too much make you fat, it

slows you down, makes you clumsy, sleepy, and dim-witted (by sending all the blood to your stomach and intestines instead of to your brain), ruins your ability to present your ideas clearly, lowers your sexual appetite, robs you of your ping, makes you dislike yourself, and does a whole lot of other things like making you susceptible to all kinds of awful health problems and diseases (like the ones caused by our modern way of life). All of which are, of course, much too unpleasant to mention in a book about power!

Eat Less, Live Longer

And to make matters worse, overeating also takes years off your life! (So why would anyone want to do it, you ask . . . .) Tests on animals show that they live longer than their expected life span when they are slightly underfed all the time. But I'm not paying homage to eating less because I want to sell you a ticket to longer life. I'm bringing this up because eating less is also a Road to Power: When you're slightly underfed, it's easier to focus. (See Chapter 8 on The Power of Focus.)

That's right. If you eat less, you will find it easier to concentrate. Why do you think so many spiritual paths include the practice of fasting? It's because fasting is a fast, effective, and dramatic way to clear your brain. If you don't believe me, just try it for three days and see what happens. When you fast, you get rid of all the excess in your life, not just food, but everything. Fasting is a real quick way to get yourself back to basics.

Don't Think About Food

I spent many years of my life studying and teaching various food techniques and disciplines for health and happiness. Raising your awareness of the relationship between food and health is always a good starting point for improving the quality of your life. But unless you have a serious illness, I suggest you move beyond that stage as fast as you can master it. Once you get the basic idea about the importance of food in your life, you know things like: 1) Cut down on animal food and fat, 2) eat less white sugar, 3) eat fewer processed foods and fewer chemicals, 4) drink less alcohol and coffee, 5) quit smoking, and 6) eat more grains, vegetables, fruits, and good bread . . . basic stuff like that. Well, once you get it, move on to the next item on your agenda.

And then don't think about food. Just forget it.

I find that not thinking about food, not focusing on it, is the best way to eat less.

Just look at people who are dieting. They are focusing so massively on food and on losing weight that it's impossible for them to do it. Because they're thinking negatively about food all the time. Oh my, what if I eat this. Oh my, look at my body. Oh my, look how terrible I look. Oh my, I'm so hungry. And all that stuff. So what they focus on increases. If you want to lose weight, forget about it. Fall in love, walk from the East Coast to the West Coast, decide to make a million this year, and I guarantee you will lose weight.

Fast and Light

The most important thing is to travel light. We talked about this before in the chapter on releasing. (See Chapter 4 on The Power of Release.) We also mentioned that the basic cause of all problems is *congestion* and that circulation is the basic cure. Well, overeating—eating more than you need to travel light—causes congestion in your mind, body, and in your life.

So as you start your releasing exercises, I suggest you add food to your releasing agenda. Let it go. Release excess food from your life and your body will revive.

The trick is to concentrate on what's important in your life and forget the rest. Before you know it, you will be eating less. Every time you think of your body, love it and bless it. Praise your body all the time. Tell it how much you appreciate it for carrying you around and digesting your food and letting you see, hear, smell, and touch the world. The body responds to praise and blessing. Not to pigging out.

And keep busy.

And enjoy the pleasure of exercising. In whatever way suits you. Just do it.

I promise you that if you're busy, if you're focusing on your dreams and plans, if you're praising and blessing your body, if you're visualizing your way to the top of whatever mountain you're climbing at the moment, you'll probably forget to eat anyway. Which is great. It'll make you faster and lighter, it'll clear your brain, your eyesight will improve, your sense of smell will be renewed, you'll enjoy living in your body so much more, you'll like exercising more, and most important of all, *you'll discover how much more powerful you are.*

Okay, you might want to pop a few vitamin pills and drink some good fresh water and eat some nice clean carrots on your way, but if you're traveling fast and light, you probably won't have time for more than that.

Chapter 16

The Power of Exercise

Besides being great fun, moving and exercising your body regularly is one of the fastest and most effective ways of raising your energy and becoming more powerful.

Most people know exercise is healthy. The benefits are obvious: better health, more energy and vitality, and a firmer, thinner, and better-looking body. But what lots of people forget, or don't know, is that exercise and movement also affect our mental, emotional, and spiritual states. I guess one of the best secret benefits of exercising is that when you move vigorously, your mind just kicks out.

Turn off Your Brain for a While

Being very brainy, thinking a lot, being very intellectual about life can be a big problem for people. Not that thinking or being an intellectual is a bad thing in itself. Problems, however, arise if you allow your intellect to dominate your life to the exclusion of your emotional and spiritual nature.

In other words, you're too brainy if you think about and analyze things, life, people, and situations so much that you don't trust your intuition anymore. If you find that you aren't listening to your own inner voice, if you don't trust those inner promptings that we all have, if you disregard your own hunches and feelings because you can't explain or justify them "logically" to yourself or to others, then it's time to watch out. Thinking and analyzing this much could be a big danger in your life because it cuts you off from so much of the intuitive information that is everywhere available about yourself and other people and about life and the nature of the universe in general.

> *The greatest war in life within each*
> *individual is between the intellect and*
> *the heart—where the heart is saying,*
> *"This is so" and the intellect is saying,*
> *"I don't understand, therefore I don't*
> *believe."*[1]
>
> EMMANUEL

The Gift of Movement
This is why physical exercise is such a gift. Physical exercise is a great way of making your mind relax its iron grip on your life. When you drench yourself in physical activity and sweat,

and/or blast yourself with fresh air, deep breathing, and the splendor of the great outdoors, you tend to stop worrying and analyzing . . . at least for a while. So it's no wonder most people feel better as soon as they get their bodies moving.

And the great thing is it doesn't matter if you throw yourself in the deep blue sea for a swim or dance like a maniac with all the shades drawn in the privacy of your own home.

Another good thing is this: Exercising your body is a physical affirmation of power, joy, and abundance. We've looked at spoken and written affirmations. (See Chapter 3 on The Power of Affirmation.) Physical exercise is another type of affirmation. An affirmation in movement, you could say! Because when you exercise, when you move your body vigorously, you are also loving, blessing, praising, and enjoying your body and the gift of life you've been given.

And of course you can reinforce physical movement by saying affirmations aloud while you exercise, which is another surefire way to increase your results tenfold.

You can declare, for example:

My body is strong, healthy, and powerful!

Perfect health is my one and only reality now!

Every day in every way my body is getting better and better!

A Power Workout

Here's a fun, energy-raising Power Workout I like. You can do it on its own or in combination with whatever other kind of exercise you like.

Step 1: Shake Your Booty!

Stand in a relaxed position with your feet planted firmly on the ground. Take a few deep breaths and relax. Start to gently shake and move your whole body. As you do, release and let go of whatever tension and tiredness you are feeling. As you gently move each part of your body, imagine that you are kindly waking up that part of your body. Start with your head and loosen up your neck gently, then move on to your shoulders, arms, fingers and hands, and back. Make whatever soft, gentle, pleasurable movements seem most natural. The goal is to relax and loosen up. Continue slowly all the way down to your toes. If you relax and take your time, you will find that each part of your body begins to loosen up and come alive again.

If you feel like it, gently shake your whole body one more time.

It's also great fun to do this exercise when you're lying down on the floor, flat on your back.

Step 2: Warm-up

Rub your hands together vigorously until you feel your palms getting warm. Then use your warm hands to warm and loosen your body from head to toe. Start at the top of your head, then move gently down to your face, neck, shoulders, stomach, legs, etc., all the way down to your toes. Take time to warm up your hands again whenever you feel they're getting too cold. When you discover a part of your body or a muscle that is tense or sore, you can spend a little extra time massaging that area of your body to help it loosen up and relax. You can even talk to your body as you massage it, telling it to relax and let go. (See Chapter 17 on The Power of Praise and Blessing.)

Step 3: Sing and Dance!

Now put on your favorite music and dance! Just let go and have some fun! Dance and move your body in whatever way you feel like, it doesn't have to look like anything special. Nobody should be watching you do this, so just relax and let go. You might want to dance real slow or real fast and crazy. Whatever suits your mood best is fine. When loosening up your body, follow your intuition; it will tell you how to move to get rid of all the kinks in your system. Don't forget, circulation is the goal.

Some people forget that music and song are also powerful affirmations, so choose your music carefully. Sometimes I'm surprised and disappointed when I discover that the words to a tune I like are very negative. It's disappointing because it means that if I keep listening to and singing a song like that, I will keep on repeating those negative affirmations, which isn't something I want to do.

Since music, songs, and words are working on a vibrational level and quickly enter our subconscious minds, it's a good idea to choose songs that are positive and life affirming if we want to feel better! So be careful when it comes to falling in love with a new song!

Step 4: Time to Sweat

After you've danced and warmed up your body (and mind), you might want to move on to some heart-thumping, heart-pumping exercise that really makes you sweat. If you don't have any particular favorite, try running for fifteen to twenty minutes in the nearest park or just keep on dancing.

Step 5: Cool Down

Finish your workout with some relaxed stretching. Start by lying on your back and allowing your breathing and pulse to slow down. You can put on some gentle, soothing music if you like. Take time to stretch every part of your body, especially those muscles you just used a lot. If you don't know any basic stretching exercises, I suggest you get yourself a good book with lots of illustrations or an exercise video. Or you might want to go to yoga or to a dance class to learn some good stretching exercises.

Step 6: Thank Your Body

You can finish your session by taking a good look at yourself in the mirror. Then thank your body for being so beautiful, serving you so well, being such a wonderful instrument, carrying you around all day long, digesting your food, taking you to the movies every once in a while, going for walks with you in the woods, making love to your partner, and whatever else you can think of. I guarantee you your body will glow with delight . . . and so will you.

Have fun!

Chapter 17

The Power of Praise and Blessing

We cannot force Good into our lives.

In fact, we can never force things on the outer plane even if sometimes it seems to be that way. When it seems possible, if you observe what happens, you will find it is only temporary.

We cannot force Good into our lives, but we can make room for the Good, first by releasing negative thoughts and emotions (see Chapter 4 on The Power of Release), and second by thinking about and dwelling upon the Good. This is because we attract whatever we dwell on.

Dwell upon the Good in Others

In every interaction with other people, we are always making choices consciously or unconsciously as to what we dwell upon. We can make a conscious choice to focus on the positive in people or situations, no matter what. In other words, we can choose to concentrate on the exciting potential of the moment and of the people involved or we can allow ourselves to dwell on everything we think is "wrong" with these people and/or this situation.

On a subconscious or vibrational level, we all pick up and perceive what other people are thinking and feeling about us. We pick up their vibrations, just as they pick up ours. Then we act and respond accordingly, usually without knowing why.

Children Love Praise

Everyone knows that children flourish and grow in amazing ways when we praise them. No matter what so-called "weaknesses/defects" we may believe a child has, if we focus our attention on the child's strengths and talents, the child will flourish. The Good will grow and in the end outshine any so-called weaknesses. Why should it be any different with us, just because we're grown-up?

Focus on the Highest and Best

The most amazing things happen when you focus on the Good in people. When you meet people, even complete strangers, and you think, feel, and act according to the highest and best in them, the situation will always move toward a more positive outcome.

Even better, you can focus on the Good in others by blessing them. Say silently, *I bless you, I bless you, I bless you,* and see what happens. You'll be surprised. It's as if your positive thoughts, your focus on the highest and best in people, and your blessings for them and to them work on the invisible, vibrational level. Without knowing it, the other person feels your blessing, feels that there is no antagonism or hostility emanating from you, which makes everything flow more smoothly and easily in the situation. Your focus on the Good can change everything.

This really works because negative thoughts and feelings create resistance on the inner plane. This resistance then manifests itself as difficulties, delays, and unexpected problems on the outer plane. But by focusing on the Highest Good and using the power of praise and blessing, you can dissolve all resistance.

Bless Your Partner

While you're at it, don't forget to bless and praise your partner in life, because this can be the greatest challenge of all. We often hold grudges, dwell on minor, unimportant details, remember old hurts, and focus on weaknesses in our partners when we would laugh at and immediately overlook, dismiss, or forgive the same in others.

To dissolve old hurts and resistance, affirm toward your partner: "_____, I bless you and behold you with the eyes of love."

Praise and Love Your Body

A great way to attract and manifest increased health and vitality is to dwell on how wonderful your body is.

Sit comfortably in your favorite chair or lie down on your back. Take a few minutes to relax. Then start at the top of your head and work your way slowly and lovingly down to your toes. Start at the top of your head and say things like, "I love my hair, my beautiful hair, which is strong, supple, and thick. The beautiful color of my hair makes it my crowning glory." Next say, "I give thanks for my eyes, my far-seeing, beautiful green eyes with which I see and enjoy all the wonders of life. . . ."

Continue downward and bless your nose, ears, mouth, teeth, face, neck, shoulders, and back. Find your own personal words of praise and blessing. If you don't have a lot of time, you can focus on different areas of your body. Say, for example, "I love and thank my heart, my strong, loving heart, for beating calmly, powerfully and regularly each and every day. And I bless my stomach for digesting my food so peacefully and easily . . ." and so forth.

Since all the universe is filled with divine intelligence, every cell of our bodies is too. As Deepak Chopra explains in his book *Ageless Body, Timeless Mind,* "The biochemistry of the body is a product of awareness. Beliefs, thoughts, and emotions create the chemical reactions that uphold life in every cell. . . . Impulses of intelligence create your body in new forms every second. What you are is the sum total of these impulses, and by changing their patterns, you will change."[1]

Talk to Your Body

Every cell of your body is responding to your thoughts at this very moment, whether the thoughts are negative or positive. So it might be a good idea to take a closer look at the way you think about your body right now.

Do you curse your body or bless it? If your thoughts are not as positive as they could be, it's never too late to change. Change your thoughts about your body and watch it respond to your new thoughts and words. From this moment on decide that whenever you think of your body, or of any part of your body, you will think of it lovingly and send it positive thoughts. Decide that from now on you will always tell your body it is strong and healthy. And praise it for all it can do. Your focus on the Good will make your body thrive.

By the same token, if any part of your body is not functioning properly or is diseased (not at ease) or is causing you pain, then talk to it as you would talk to a child you love and cherish. (Do you not love and cherish your own body?) So have a nice talk with that part of your body. If you have a stomachache, have a little chat with your stomach. Say, "Dear stomach, why are you so upset today? What's the problem? Did I eat something that doesn't agree with you? Or is something eating you? Am I too tense for your liking? Am I rushing around too much? Did I drink too much coffee?" Then listen to the answers . . . listen to your intuition and take heed of what it says.

And don't forget to end your little conversation by saying, "Dear stomach, I really love you and bless you and thank you for the wonderful work you are doing each and every day . . . digesting food and emotions and ideas . . . you are most amazing, dear stomach. So now you can just relax. Yes, just let go and relax. Release all the pain and tension. I see every single one of your cells, dear stomach, now filled with radiant life force and shining white light. And I know that you are now feeling much, much better. Yes, right here and right now." And so it is.

Writing to the Higher Self

Writing to the Higher Self is another wonderful "praise and blessing" technique. If you are having problems with someone on the outer plane and are finding it is difficult to talk to the person or reason with him or her, then try writing to the person's Higher Self. It's a good way to bring harmony to the situation.

Since the Higher Self is the true spiritual self of every person, when you focus on a person's Higher Self, you are focusing on all that is true, good, and real about that person. Moreover, you are activating the positive energy of this soul by the focus of your attention.

I find writing to someone's Higher Self is a very comforting thing to do when there is disharmony between you on the outer plane. Somehow, when you write to the Higher Self of someone who troubles you, you are sending your love and blessings directly to the other person's soul, bypassing their ego. This is good because the ego is the cause of so much interpersonal strife, conflict, and misunderstanding.

When you write directly from your heart to another person's Higher Self, be loving and be specific. Ask the Higher Self to help manifest the Highest Good for all in the situation that is troubling you. Keep writing to this person's Higher Self every day until the situation clears up. You may be surprised at what happens. Just remember, you can never ask the Higher Self for anything less than the Highest Good for everyone involved.

You can also write to the Higher Self of your friends or loved ones when you are worried about them. For example, if someone close to you is ill or you feel they need strength and support to face a difficult challenge in their life, ask the Higher Self to guide and protect this person. Or decree: "I call upon the Higher Self of ___ to protect ___ on her way (in this situation)."

You can also write to the Higher Self of your children or to your own Higher Self. And you can call upon your own Higher Self to protect you in times of distress, just as you would call upon God, Jesus Christ, Buddha, angelic or other high spiritual beings for protection.

As with affirmations, you will gain power, strength, and a sense of peace by repeating your decrees aloud many times on a daily basis, until you feel the problem has been dissolved.

Chapter 18

The Power of Friends

As true friends, we can work wonders for each other.

When we are in the midst of a crisis or facing some big problem, it may seem difficult to see the Highest Good and to maintain this vision of the Highest Good, no matter what is happening on the outer plane. This happens because we are too close to the situation. We are too involved emotionally with what's happening to keep in touch with (to keep focused on) the highest, most loving universal perspective. Unfortunately, when our egos get involved in crisis or conflict like this, we may get sucked into our own fears, anxieties, resentments, doubts, and worries, especially when we are new on the Road to Power.

But a good friend can help.

A good friend is invaluable at times like this.

A good friend can make all the difference.

A good friend can turn the tide.

A good friend is a Godsend.

Everyone should have a good friend whom one

can ask to speak words of truth (say positive affirmations) on one's behalf in times of crisis or when in need.

As Florence Scovel Shinn explains in her book *The Game of Life and How to Play It*, "In this instance the man could never have demonstrated alone. He needed someone to help him hold to the vision. This is what one man can do for another. . . . The friend or 'healer' sees clearly the success, health, or prosperity, and never wavers, because he is not close to the situation. It is much easier to 'demonstrate' for someone else than for one's self, so a person should not hesitate to ask for help, if he feels himself wavering."[1]

Ask Your Friend

I strongly advise asking a close friend to speak words declaring positive results for you when you are in need. For example, when you face an unusual or difficult situation, ask your friend to affirm a successful outcome for you. (See Chapter 3 on The Power of Affirmation and Chapter 17 on The Power of Praise and Blessing.) Your friend can affirm for you:

_____ (name), the job interview is a great success. You are relaxed and present yourself in the best possible way.

_____ (name), the operation is a complete success. You recover quickly and are healthier than ever before.

_____ (name), I know you give birth to a healthy child peacefully and easily.

_____ (name), you are definitely capable of this task. You have the talent to do the job. I see you going from success to success with this project.

And obviously we can do the same for our friends. In fact, I believe we should not hesitate to speak words of power for our friends, even if they are too shy to ask for our help and even in cases when our friends don't share our view of life or realize exactly what we are doing.

Listen to your intuition and you will know when you are needed. Then dare to turn the tide for your friend by speaking bold words of success!

The Master Mind Group

You can also join forces with one or more of your friends to achieve definite goals. Napoleon Hill calls the power that is generated when like-minded people join together the power of the "Master Mind." He defines the "Master Mind" concept as: "Coordination of knowledge and effort, in a spirit of harmony, between two or more people, for the attainment of a definite purpose."[2]

Hill suggests that if properly chosen, a group of like-minded people can become a "Master Mind" group and achieve great Good when everyone focuses their energy on the same goal. "When a group of individual brains are coordinated and function in harmony, the increased energy created through that alliance becomes available to every individual brain in the group."[3] Of course, we all do this, often unconsciously, and many successful undertakings are the result of like-minded people working in harmony toward common goals. But when you're on the Road to Power, you can consciously use this technique and create or join a "Master Mind" group to achieve your goals.

Join Together and Affirm

In like manner, we can join together to pray for, bless, or make affirmations for others. For example, a family can join together to affirm or visualize a positive outcome for a sick relative, friend, or family member. Likewise, if one person in the family is facing a difficult challenge, the whole family can join together and affirm success for the individual. Family affirmations don't have to be a big deal or take a long time. Affirmations can be said at the dinner table or at some other appropriate time when everyone is present.

Or you might want to join a prayer group. Usually prayer groups work like this: Everyone in the prayer group brings his or her prayer list to the meeting. The list can be a list of people one wishes to bless or pray for or it can be a list of positive results one wants to manifest. These prayer lists are personal and secret. Everyone keeps their lists to themselves, but everyone in the group prays or affirms together for all the people or positive results on the lists.

As with the "Master Mind" concept, when people join together to make positive affirmations, the power to manifest Good is greatly increased. So let us not hesitate to work together for the Highest Good of everyone.

Chapter 19

The Power of Fast Food for the soul

Let's admit it. You're reading this book because you want change, you want a better life—and you want it now. The title of this book caught your eye because not only do you want to reclaim your power over your life, you want to reclaim it as fast as possible.

You've experienced that feeling of "divine" discontent long enough and now you want practical tools that can help you change things. You want to know most specifically how to create the Life you know deep in your heart you should be living.

And that's just great. Because it's precisely this feeling of "divine" discontent that has driven you to search for something more, for something better. And here you sit with this book in your hands—with its techniques and insights into the way the mind works, in short with precisely the tools you need. So congratulations!

If anybody had told me just a few short years ago that the simple techniques described in this book would totally transform my life—and vastly improve it—I would have laughed and said, sure. But it just so happens that they did, which is why I know they can do the same for you.

The Way the Mind Works
The real key to change is understanding the way the mind works. And now you've got that key in your hand. Now you know that your thoughts, words, and mental pictures are creating your reality; you know that what you affirm and visualize will become your Life. You also know that you are the only thinker in your mind—so you're the only one who can decide what you are going to think and focus your attention on. And this is the key to freedom!

With this magical key in hand—and the practical techniques described in this book—you have what it takes to totally transform your Life. And take it from me, it's easy to do!

Why Shouldn't It Be Easy?
One of the main messages of this book is that it's easy to live a healthy, happy, prosperous Life, even though we may have been programmed to believe otherwise. An unhappy, impoverished life

is the result of our own ignorance; it's the result of our own negative mental patterns, the manifestation of our own thoughts, words, and focus on limitation. And since most people don't understand the way the mind works—how their thoughts and words are creating their reality—they are victims of their own negative thinking.

But once we understand the mechanism, we also understand that the good Life, the healthy Life, the productive, useful Life—the Life of unlimited vitality, love, and exciting adventures—is our natural birthright. We realize we just forgot how to bring it forth. But now we know how to do it.

Do the Inner Work

There is, however, one condition. With this new knowledge in hand, we must be willing to do the inner work. We must be willing to take a closer look at our attitudes and mental programs, and be ruthlessly honest with ourselves. What are we thinking, what are our basic attitudes toward Life? What are we saying to ourselves and to other people on a regular basis? Are our thoughts and words good enough? Are they positive enough, kind enough, loving enough? Will they create the kind of Life, the kind of world, the kind of reality we really want . . . for ourselves and for our families, friends, and fellow human beings?

The Road to Power

So you decide.

It's up to you! You can claim your own power now. You can take control of your thoughts, words, and the focus of your attention and consciously create the Life you want to live.

The tools are right here. The way before you is wide open.

So be bold. Be brave. Take control of your destiny now. Think for yourself—and get going.

Nobody else can do it for you.

Nobody else can take it from you.

This is the Road to Power.

Chapter 3

1. John 1:1, The Holy Bible, King James Version (New York: Meridian, 1974).
2. Emile Coué, quoted by Brian Inglis and Ruth West, *The Alternative Health Guide* (London: Mermaid Books, 1983).

Chapter 5

1. Catherine Ponder, *The Dynamic Laws of Healing* (Marina Del Rey, CA: DeVorrs & Company, 1985).
2. Deepak Chopra, *Creating Health* (Boston: Houghton Mifflin Company, 1991).
3. Norman Cousins, *Anatomy of an Illness As Perceived by the Patient* (New York: Bantam Doubleday Dell, 1991).
4. Ibid.
5. Deepak Chopra, *Ageless Body, Timeless Mind* (New York: Harmony Books, 1993).
6. Ibid.
7. Anthony Robbins, *Awaken the Giant Within* (New York: Fireside, 1992).

Chapter 6

1. Napoleon Hill, *Think and Grow Rich* (New York: Fawcett Crest, 1960).

2. Deepak Chopra, *Ageless Body, Timeless Mind* (New York: Harmony Books, 1993).
3. Catherine Ponder, *The Dynamic Laws of Healing* (Marina Del Rey, CA: DeVorrs & Company, 1985).

Chapter 7
1. José Silva, *You the Healer* (Tiburon, CA: HJ Kramer Inc., 1989).

Chapter 8
1. *Webster's Encyclopedic Unabridged Dictionary* (New York: Portland House, 1989).
2. Deepak Chopra, *Ageless Body, Timeless Mind* (New York: Harmony Books, 1993).
3. Stuart Wilde, *Affirmations* (Taos, NM: White Dove International, 1989).
4. Emmet Fox, *Power Through Constructive Thinking* (San Francisco: HarperSanFrancisco, 1979).
5. Napoleon Hill, *Think and Grow Rich* (New York: Fawcett Crest, 1960).
6. Ibid.
7. Ibid.

Chapter 10
1. Emmet Fox, *Alter Your Life* (San Francisco: HarperSanFrancisco, 1994).

Chapter 12
1. Emmet Fox, *Power Through Constructive Thinking* (San Francisco: HarperSanFrancisco, 1979).
2. Pat Rodegast and Judith Stanton, *Emmanuel's Book* (New York: Bantam Books, 1987).

Chapter 16
1. Ibid

Chapter 17
   1. Deepak Chopra, *Ageless Body, Timeless Mind* (New York: Harmony Books, 1993).

Chapter 18
   1. Florence Scovel Shinn, *The Game of Life and How to Play It* (New York: Simon & Schuster, 1989).
   2. Napoleon Hill, *Think and Grow Rich* (New York: Fawcett Crest, 1960).
   3. Ibid.

About the Author

American author Barbara Berger describes herself as "a sincere seeker, a passionate student of metaphysics, and a hip businesswoman and communicator." Her mission is to communicate in contemporary lingo her unique blend of cutting-edge mental technologies and ancient wisdom, designed to empower readers in their endeavors to improve life for themselves and their communities.

Barbara Berger grew up in Bethesda, Maryland, and attended Sarah Lawrence College. After a tumultuous youth and years of world travel, she married a Dane and settled in Copenhagen, Denmark, where she and her husband owned and ran a health center in downtown Copenhagen. When the marriage ended in the mid 1980s, Barbara found herself in a foreign country, a single parent of three growing boys—with no means of support. Using the techniques described in *Fast Food for the Soul,* she turned her life around. She now heads her own communications firm, Barbara Berger Communications, which specializes in corporate communications and deals with many of Denmark's leading companies. In 1995, she started a publishing house, BeamTeam Books, which publishes books, tapes, and music.

Barbara has written more than ten books that are widely published in Scandinavia and the rest of Europe.

For more information about Barbara Berger and her activities, contact:

BeamTeam Books
Livjaegergade 19 st tv
2100 Copenhagen O
Denmark
Telephone: (+45) 35 26 51 55
Fax: (+45) 35 26 50 88
Email: beamteam@beamteam.com
Web site: www.beamteam.com